GREATEST MOMENTS OF

RUGBY

6440326.

GREATEST MOMENTS OF
RUGBY

First published in the UK in 2007

© G2 Entertainment Limited 2014

www.G2ent.co.uk

Printed and bound in Europe

ISBN 978-1-782812-62-3

CONTENTS

THE BRITISH LIONS WIN IN NEW ZEALAND
1971

While the British Lions had registered two previous victories over the New Zealand All Blacks – 6-3 in June 1930 and 9-6 in September 1959 – the 34-man squad that ventured to the southern hemisphere in 1971 was to surpass all expectations.

Although combined British and Irish teams had participated in unofficial tours of Australia and New Zealand since 1888, it was not until 1930 that the Lions officially engaged the All Blacks on their home turf. The first Lions tour with players selected from all four Home Nations took place in South Africa in 1910 but it was not until the inter-war years that the team became known as the Lions, so named after the crest on their jerseys.

Coach Carwyn James built the core of the team around the backbone of the Wales side that had won that year's Five Nations Grand Slam with John Dawes, JPR Williams, Gerald Davies, Mike Gibson, Gareth Edwards and Barry John appearing in all four Tests. In total, 14 Welshmen were selected for the squad, with eight from England and six each from Scotland and Ireland.

In the early stages of the first Test in Dunedin, scrum-half Gareth Edwards limped off to be replaced by fellow Welshman Ray "Chico" Hopkins who went on to play out of his skin. The first points of the game came when the Lions won a line-out and the ball eventually found its way into the hands of John Bevan, who crashed through the New Zealand defence before spilling the ball. When Alan Sutherland attempted to clear his line, Scottish loosehead prop Ian "Mighty Mouse" McLaughlan was there to charge the ball down and claim a try for the visitors. Although fly-half Barry John failed with the conversion, it was his kicking that kept the tourists in the game. As well as helping relieve the pressure on his defence with quality balls down the line, he successfully kicked two penalties to give the Lions a 9-3 victory after full-back Fergie McCormick had equalised for New Zealand with another penalty kick.

The second Test, a fortnight later, saw the All Blacks gain revenge for the opening defeat with a 22-12 triumph although the Lions scored a classic try when full-back JPR Williams collected a high New Zealand clearance deep in his own half. Immediately launching a counterattack, Williams

THE BRITISH LIONS WIN IN NEW ZEALAND

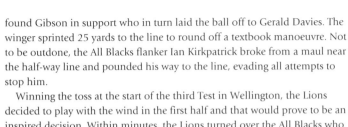

found Gibson in support who in turn laid the ball off to Gerald Davies. The winger sprinted 25 yards to the line to round off a textbook manoeuvre. Not to be outdone, the All Blacks flanker Ian Kirkpatrick broke from a maul near the half-way line and pounded his way to the line, evading all attempts to stop him.

Winning the toss at the start of the third Test in Wellington, the Lions decided to play with the wind in the first half and that would prove to be an inspired decision. Within minutes, the Lions turned over the All Blacks who had won a line-out near their goal-line and Gerald Davies scored the first try of the game. Minutes later, a line-out in nearly the same position on the right wing was palmed down by John Taylor into the path of Gareth Edwards. He jinked past a couple of New Zealand challenges before handing the ball to Barry John for an easy try by the post. With John converting the two tries and adding a drop goal, the score at the end of the first half stood at 13-0 to the Lions. In the second half, the Lions restricted the All Blacks to one try, scored by full-back Laurie Mains. This victory meant that the Lions could not now lose the series and had everything to play for in the fourth and final Test.

Things started well for the All Blacks in Auckland when Wayne Cottrell powered over the line to score the first try of the game. Main successfully kicked the conversion and added a penalty to give the home side an 8-0 lead. But the Lions were not out of the contest and flanker Peter Dixon reduced the deficit, scoring a try just before half-time with Barry John restoring parity with the conversion and a penalty by the interval.

Shortly after the game had restarted, John gave the visitors the lead with another penalty before Tom Lister scored the All Blacks' second try to level the scores at 11 apiece. It was full-back JPR Williams who stunned the watching world when he attempted a drop goal from just inside his opponents' half. The 45-yard kick flew straight between the posts and for the last 25 minutes the Lions were forced to defend against the All Black tide. As it turned out, the only score they could add was a Mains penalty to level at 14-14 and the visitors rejoiced at the end of the match, having won the series 2-1.

THE DAY THE PUBS RAN DRY
1972

It is hard enough for an international side to beat the mighty All Blacks, let alone a club side. So when Welsh club Llanelli took on New Zealand on 31 October 1972, few were predicting that the visitors would do anything other than emerge victorious.

New Zealand had recently registered a hat-trick of wins over a touring Australia side and hadn't lost a match on tour since they were beaten 17-20 by South Africa in Johannesburg more than two years previously. Indeed, their 1972 tour of North America, the British Isles and France had got off to a spectacular start with convincing victories over British Columbia (31-3), New York Metropolitan (41-9) and Western Counties (39-12).

Llanelli were coached by Carwyn James, their former fly-half and the man who had masterminded the British Lions' successful tour of New Zealand the previous year. James, born the son of a coalminer in 1929, was a Welsh international who had played two games for his country in 1958 but who would undoubtedly have won more caps if Cliff Morgan hadn't been the resident fly-half. James was a strong believer in the old adage that attack is the best form of defence and he instilled an attitude in his teams that once they got hold of the ball they should go on the offensive. Off the field, James stood as a Plaid Cymru candidate in Llanelli in the 1970 General Election and the BBC Wales Sports Personality of the Year Award has since been named in his honour.

With a 1967 victory against Australia already under their belt, Llanelli welcomed a crowd of more than 20,000 to Stradey Park – a stadium that will be covered with 400 houses after 2007 – to witness what would turn out to be a Halloween spectacular. It seemed as if the whole town had shut down for the afternoon.

The team line-up that day was: Roger Davies, John J Williams, Roy Bergiers, Ray Gravell, Andy Hill, Phil Bennett, Chico Hopkins, Tony Crocker, Roy Thomas, Barry Llewellyn, Delme Thomas, Derek Quinnell, Tom David, Hefin Jenkins and Gareth Jenkins.

Soon after the match kicked off, the home side had the chance to take an early lead when the referee awarded a penalty after only four minutes. The crowd waited with baited breath as Phil

THE DAY THE PUBS RAN DRY

Bennett stepped up to the ball only to see his kick rebound off the crossbar. All Black Linsey Colling collected the ball and seemed certain to kick for safety and clear his lines but Llanelli were already closing him down.

They had practised following up Bennett's kicks on the training ground with centre Roy Bergiers sprinting towards one post and winger JJ Williams heading for the other. This time, it was Bergiers who got there first and charged down the scrum-half's attempted clearance. Then it was just a matter of diving onto the loose ball to score a try and give the home side the lead.

Bergiers, a local teacher at that time, remembers "I just managed to get a hand to it and got a beautiful bounce. I dived on the ball and the whole place went bananas. I looked up and all the students from the school where I taught were leaping about behind the posts."

Bennett converted the try to give Llanelli a shock 6-0 lead but it wasn't long before they were to feel the full might of the All Blacks. It was a bruising encounter, as flanker Gareth Jenkins explained: "It was the most physical game I've ever played in – we'd never experienced anything like it as younger players."

Nevertheless, captain Delme Thomas steadied his pack and withstood one onslaught after another. But when full-back Joe Karam reduced the deficit to three points with a well-taken penalty kick, it seemed to many that the floodgates were about to open. But Llanelli held firm, showing their determination not to be overawed or over-run by their opponents and it was late in the second half before any further points were scored.

This time, they went to the home side when winger Andy Hill successfully kicked a long-range penalty. The Scarlets held on to record a thrilling and unbelievable 9-3 victory over New Zealand, a feat that was later immortalised in Max Boyce's song "9-3".

The players were carried off the pitch by the jubilant fans and the whole town celebrated well into the night. In fact, they celebrated so much that the pubs in the village sold out of beer. Gareth Jenkins – currently head coach of Wales' national team – allegedly took the next week off work at the steel plant where he earned his living to celebrate!

Llanelli have beaten other international sides in the intervening years, with Australia being dispatched in 1984 and 1992 while the Fijian touring side left Stradey Park empty-handed in 1985.

BARBARIANS SCORE THE TRY OF THE CENTURY
1973

When the Barbarians took on New Zealand at Cardiff Arms Park on 27 January 1973, many hoped for a repeat performance of the British Lions' victory two years earlier but few were expecting such a marvellous game. While the All Blacks were still a major force to be reckoned with, they had already lost three games – against Llanelli 3-9, North-Western Counties 14-16 and Midlands Counties (West) 8-16 – on their tour of North America, the British Isles and France.

For many people, mention of this game brings to mind the try that was scored after the first few minutes that has since been labelled the Try of the Century or simply the Try. But that is not the whole story of the game, a game that has been acclaimed as one of the best examples of attacking and counterattacking rugby the world has ever seen. "People tend only to remember the first four minutes of the game because of the try," confesses Gareth Edwards, "but what they forgot is the great deal of good rugby played afterwards, much of which came from the All Blacks."

The Barbarians are an invitational rugby team, where the only qualifications are that the player is of a sufficiently high standard and that he has behaved himself both on and off the pitch. The concept had come from William Percy Carpmael in 1890 and the Baa Baas' first game was a 9-4 victory over Hartlepool Rovers on 27 December. There is traditionally one uncapped player picked in every team and, while the players wear their own club socks, the team play in black and white hoops.

The club's motto – "Rugby Football is a game for gentleman in all classes, but for no bad sportsman in any class" – was given to the club by original member and former Bishop of Bloemfontein WJ Carey and all players concur that becoming a Barbarian is one of the greatest achievements in the game. The club's philosophy is one of an attacking game with plenty of flowing rugby and lots of tries.

In 1948, the Home Unions asked the Barbarians to put together a team to play the touring Australia and the Final Challenge was born, traditionally the last match played by an Australian, New Zealand or South African side visiting this country. And so, on 27 January 1973, the

Barbarians faced their Final Challenge. The preparations for the game had not gone well for the Barbarians, with players unusually dropping passes in training, and both Gerald Davies and Mervyn Davies had to withdraw through injury and illness.

Following some early skirmishes the All Blacks cleared the ball and Phil Bennett collected it in front of his own posts. Starting off on a jinking run, he soon unloaded the ball to JPR Williams who managed to release the ball to John Pullin as he was tackled. He passed to John Dawes who set off towards the All Black line before passing to the uncapped Tom David. He threw the ball to Derek Quinnell who looked to be passing to David Buckham but Gareth Edwards collected the ball at speed and sprinted the rest of the way to the try-line to put the Barbarians 4-0 up.

Although Phil Bennett failed with the conversion, the Baa Baas continued to rack up the points in the first half. On the half-hour mark, Bennett scored a penalty from 25 yards before they scored their second try of the game when Furgus Slattery collected a loose ball from New Zealand's scrum 10 yards out and touched down to make it 11-0. Bennett again converted and, two minutes later, it was John Bevan who fended off several All Black challenges to score the Barbarians third try and send them into the half-time interval with a 17-0 lead.

The All Blacks hit back following the break with a 25-yard penalty from full-back Joe Karam after Edwards had been penalised for not feeding the ball straight into the scrum. Two minutes later, winger Grant Batty was on the end of an All Black move that had come from winning a Barbarians line-out to score a try that reduced the deficit to 10 points. It was Batty who scored New Zealand's second try with 10 minutes to go, brilliantly rounding John Dawes before chipping the ball round JPR Williams.

The final try of the game was the epitome of what the Barbarians' rugby is all about. After a series of penetrating runs by David Duckham, Mike Gibson and Furgus Slattery, JPR Williams was on hand to carry the ball into the corner to seal the victory. Bennett converted to give the Baa Baas a 23-11 triumph over the All Blacks that everyone who attended the match will remember for the rest of their lives.

WALES WIN THEIR SECOND GRAND SLAM IN THREE YEARS 1978

The 1970s were the heyday of Welsh rugby, with the Red Dragons claiming four Five Nations titles in five years between 1975-79. In two of those campaigns, 1976 and 1978, they also completed the Grand Slam with victories over England, Ireland, Scotland and France.

The players who proudly wore the red jersey of their home nation were also pivotal in the successes enjoyed during that decade by the British Lions and the Barbarians. Names like Gareth Edwards, Phil Bennett and JPR Williams are not just written in Welsh history but in that of the British Isles as a whole.

It was the era when there were only two matches played on each weekend with one team resting. The opening weekend saw Wales as the odd ones out as Ireland beat Scotland 12-9 and France triumphed over England 15-6.

The second matchday saw Wales head to Twickenham in a game that celebrated Edwards' 50th cap. Edwards had first played for Wales in 1967 at the age of 17 and three years later he was captaining the side. He would win 53 caps before his retirement from international rugby at the end of the 1978 season, a remarkable achievement made even more amazing by the fact that his caps were won in successive games…such was his consistency.

On a waterlogged pitch, it was perhaps inevitable that neither side would be able to score a try and by half-time England were leading 6-3 thanks to two penalties from Alistair Hignell. After the interval, Phil Bennett added two penalties to the one he had earlier converted in the first half to give Wales a hard-fought 9-6 victory. In the other game on matchday two, France kept their title hopes alive with a close-fought 19-16 victory at Murrayfield.

The third weekend saw Wales host Scotland at Cardiff Arms Park in a match notable for Gareth Edwards scoring his 20th and final try in a Wales jersey. With the half-time score being Wales 8 Scotland 7, the home team picked up the pace in the second half to emerge 22-14 victors. The Scots had scored two tries to Wales' four: Alan Tomes, a rugby colossus at 6ft 5in and 17 stone and Jim Renwick – each converted by captain Doug Morgan. Derek Quinnell (father of two future

WALES WIN THEIR SECOND GRAND SLAM IN THREE YEARS

Welsh internationals in Scott and Craig), Ray Gravell and Steve Fenwick registered touchdowns along with Edwards. Quinnell's try would be his only one for his country.

Meanwhile, Wales' main contenders for the Grand Slam, France, kept pace with their title rivals with a 10-9 victory over Ireland. By half-time, France were leading through a Jerome Gallion try and two penalties from the boot of Jean-Michael Aguirre while Ireland's Tony Ward had replied with two penalties himself. Ward would add a third successful kick in the second half but the Irish were unable to register any more points.

Wales became the first country to secure a third consecutive Triple Crown, with a 20-16 victory over Ireland at Lansdowne Road (Irish legend Mike Gibson was making a world-record 64th Test appearance). Leading half-time by 13-6, Wales held their resolve in the face of an Irish onslaught after the interval. In the end, tries from Steve Fenwick – plus four penalties – and JJ Williams proved sufficient against an Irish side that could only score one try (John Moloney) and four Tony Ward kicks (three penalties and a drop goal). In that weekend's other game, England thrashed Scotland 15-0 at Murrayfield with tries from Barry Nelmes and Peter Squires. A Paul Dodge penalty and two Malcolm Young conversions made up the points tally.

The Grand Slam hinged on what unbeaten France could achieve on their arrival in Cardiff. The visitors drew first blood with a Jean-Claude Skrela try and Bernard Vivies' drop goal earning the Cockerels a 7-0 lead. Wales, however, fought back and put their first points on the board when Phil Bennett sidestepped a challenge to score a try in the corner and successfully kicked the resulting conversion. The home side raced into a 13-7 lead before half-time with an Edwards drop goal and Bennett's second try of the match. The only score in the second half was another drop goal, this time from Steve Fenwick which gave Wales a 16-7 victory and the Grand Slam title.

Although it was not announced prior to the fixture, this match marked the international retirement of Phil Bennett (aged 29) and Gareth Edwards (30) and, with Gerald Davies (33) also hanging up his boots, Wales lost a vital ingredient of what had made them so successful. Welsh rugby went into decline during the 1980s and 1990s and they would have to wait another 27 years to claim a further Grand Slam title.

ENGLAND WIN THE TITLE OUTRIGHT
1980

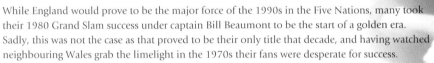

While England would prove to be the major force of the 1990s in the Five Nations, many took their 1980 Grand Slam success under captain Bill Beaumont to be the start of a golden era. Sadly, this was not the case as that proved to be their only title that decade, and having watched neighbouring Wales grab the limelight in the 1970s their fans were desperate for success.

England had been in the doldrums in the 1970s, failing to win a single game in 1972 and 1976 and winning just one game in 1974, 1975 and 1979. The 1972 season could not be completed due to the troubles in Ireland and the 1973 championship was shared between England, France, Ireland, Scotland and Wales as each of the five teams ended the campaign with two victories to their name.

The last match of the 1980 Five Nations tournament saw England travel to face Scotland at Murrayfield. Captain Bill Beaumont and his team knew that victory would mean England's first Five Nations championship since 1963, and their first Grand Slam since 1957.

The campaign had begun well with a 24-9 victory over Ireland at Twickenham. Mike Slemen, Steve Smith and John Scott scored a try apiece with Dusty Hare adding three conversions and two penalties while Ireland could only reply with three penalties from Ollie Campbell. The other fixture of the opening weekend saw Wales beat France by 18-9.

England's second match of the season saw them travel to Parc des Princes to take on 1977 Grand Slam champions France. It was a much more closely fought encounter than England's previous fixture with both sides scoring two tries. France's came from captain Jean-Pierre Rives and Jean-Luc Averous while John Carleton and Nick Preston touched down for England. In the end, the difference between the two teams would prove to be kicking with Alain Caussade successfully slotting a conversion and a penalty through the posts. England, however, could rely on Dusty Hare (one penalty) and John Horton (two drop goals) to compete their scoring and claim a 17-13 triumph. In the other match, Ireland conquered Scotland by 22-15.

The following matchday paired England with Wales and it proved to be a very tight affair at Twickenham with England emerging 9-8 victors. Although the visitors scored the only two tries of

the game through Elgan Rees and Jeff Squire, they had to play the last hour with 14 men after flanker Paul Ringer was sent off for a late tackle. Dusty Hare converted the last of his three penalty kicks in the dying minutes to dash Wales' hopes of a fifth consecutive Triple Crown. Ireland had the weekend off, as Scotland overcame France 22-14 at Murrayfield.

It was England's turn to watch the other games the following matchday and they would have been extremely happy with the results as, with Wales beating Scotland 17-6 and France edging out Ireland 19-18, it meant they went into their final match knowing they were already going to be crowned Five Nations champions. It just remained to be seen as to whether they could claim the Grand Slam as well.

As Ireland beat Wales 21-7 at Lansdowne Road, England were taking on the auld enemy, Scotland, for the 1980 Calcutta Cup. This cup had been presented to the RFU in 1878, having been crafted from silver that had been melted down from silver rupees owned by the now-defunct Calcutta Club in India. It was first played for the following year and, as the original is kept locked away in a vault, replicas are held by both the RFU and SRU.

The match turned out to be a classic with England unstoppable in the first half. In his first international season, young centre Clive Woodward was really making a name for himself. He ran rings around the Scots and set up the first two tries for Carleton and Slemen which Hare duly converted. A scrum in the corner seemed to be heading over Scotland's goal-line when Scott and Smith contrived to give Carleton the opportunity to score his second try of the game. Three penalties followed before half-time, two to Scotland's Irvine and one to Hare, giving England a 19-3 lead.

Just eight minutes after the restart, Smith scored his side's fourth try and, as the second half drew on, it looked like the hosts could pull themselves back into the game but it was not to be. Despite Rutherford and Tomes registering tries for Scotland, Carleton completed his hat-trick and England won by 30-18 to claim their first Grand Slam in 23 years.

Beaumont's heroes remain the only English side to ever win the Grand Slam on Scottish soil, an accomplishment made much sweeter by the fact it was won against their fiercest rivals.

IRELAND WIN FIVE NATIONS 1982

The 1982 Five Nations championship was notable on two accounts: firstly, Ireland won their first Triple Crown since 1949 and secondly, Wales lost at home for the first time since the 9-14 defeat to France in 1968. For a team used to success – the only other team to secure the Triple Crown in the 1960s and 1970s was England in 1960 – this was a disaster, and set the Red Dragons on the rocky road to ruin that would take them years to recover from.

The Triple Crown is awarded to whichever Home Nation team, out of England, Ireland, Scotland and Wales, wins their matches against the other three. Although France and now Italy also compete in the same tournament, they are not eligible for the Triple Crown. The Crown – albeit mythical, because there wasn't actually a physical trophy until 2006 – was first contested in 1883 and England have won it a record 23 times. In 1975, a retired coalminer named Dave Marrington whittled away at a lump of coal to produce a work of art that was mounted on a four-sided plinth bearing a rose, a shamrock, a thistle and the Prince of Wales feathers but the Home Nations decided against awarding this as a trophy and so it now resides in Twickenham's Museum of Rugby.

The first match in the 1982 tournament saw Scotland and England play out a 9-9 draw at Murrayfield. In a match dominated by kicking, there wasn't a single try scored. Andy Irvine converted two penalties for the Scots with John Rutherford adding a drop goal while Marcus Rose and Paul Dodge scored one and two penalties respectively.

The following weekend, Ireland played host to Wales and saw off the challenge of the red tide. Leading at half-time by 9-8, Wales found points harder to come by in the second half and Ireland eventually won the game 20-12 with tries from Trevor Ringland (1) and Moss Finn (2) with Ollie Campbell completing the scoring for the home side with a conversion and a penalty. Terry Holmes (one try), Gwyn Evans (one conversion, one penalty) and Gary Pearce (a drop goal) notched the points for the visitors.

Wales made amends when France visited Cardiff Arms Park, running out 22-12 winners with another try from Holmes and six penalties from Evans. The only French try was scored by a young

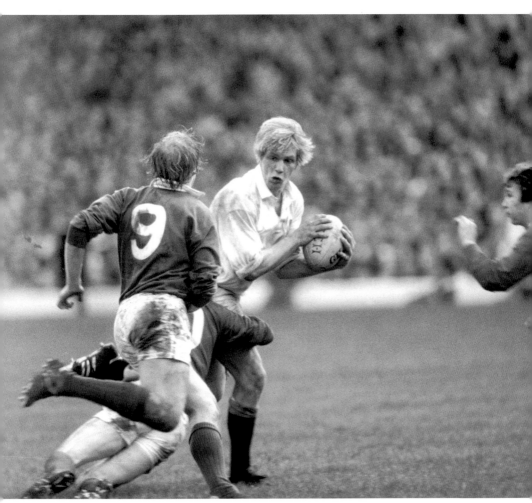

Serge Blanco. In the other match that weekend, England entertained Ireland at Twickenham but lost 15-16 despite a Mike Slemen try and a conversion plus three penalties from Rose. Hugo MacNeill and Ginger McLaughlin touched down the two Irish tries with Campbell adding another eight points from his boot.

The next opponents to face Ireland – coached by Tom Kiernan and captained by Ciaran Fitzgerald – at Lansdowne Road were the unbeaten Scottish side. An Irish team had never won the Triple Crown at Lansdowne Road so much was expected of their heroes who had the chance to triumph for the first time since 1949. While the visitors applied the pressure with a Rutherford try, an Irvine conversion and two Jim Renwick penalties, it was Ollie Campbell who was named man of the match after scoring all Ireland's 21 points. He kicked six penalty goals and a drop goal to give Ireland their first Crown in 33 years.

The same weekend, England overcame the mighty French Cockerels to register an impressive 27-15 victory. John Carleton and a certain Clive Woodward – who would be knighted after leading England to World Cup triumph in 2003 – scored the English tries with Laurent Pardo crossing the line for the only French touchdown. Dusty Hare was in fine form for the visitors, kicking two conversions and five penalties.

England completed their campaign with a 17-7 victory over Wales while Scotland were beating France 16-7. Carleton and Slemen were again on the scoresheet for England while Rutherford proved his reliability with yet another try for Scotland.

The final weekend of the tournament saw Scotland condemn Wales to the wooden spoon with a 34-18 victory at Cardiff Arms Park with tries from Jim Pollock, Jim Calder, David Johnston, Derek White and Fenwick. The Scots became the first visiting team to score five tries in an international in Cardiff as Wales' 14-year-old unbeaten home record in the Five Nations came to an end. In the aftermath, coach John Lloyd was sacked and it would be another 12 years before Wales won both their home championship games in a season.

Ireland travelled to France looking for their first Grand Slam since 1948, but Campbell's three penalties were not sufficient to realise the Irish dream. Tries from Blanco and Patrick Mesny gave France a relatively comfortable 22-9 win. Ireland had some consolation, however, in their first Five Nations title since 1974.

FRANCE TRIUMPH OVER AUSTRALIA 30-24
1987

With the football World Cup having been in existence since 1930, it was high time that Rugby Union's equivalent took place and, while the idea had been mooted in the early 1980s, the inaugural competition was jointly hosted by Australia and New Zealand in 1987. Organised by the game's ruling body, the International Rugby Board, the event is now held every four years.

Seven of the 16 places in the initial competition went to IRB members Australia, New Zealand, England, France, Ireland, Scotland and Wales. South Africa were unable to participate due to the boycott because of Apartheid. The other nine places were filled by invitation.

The format of the competition saw the 16 teams divided into pools of four with the top two in each group progressing to the knockout stages. Such was the advantage that the seven major sides held over the nine minor nations that the crowds witnessed several high-scoring games, including New Zealand 70 Italy 6, New Zealand 74 Fiji 13 and France 70 Zimbabwe 12. It was no surprise, therefore, when the eight teams who made it through to the knockout stage were Australia, England, Wales, Ireland, France, Scotland, New Zealand and Fiji (the latter qualified with a better points difference than Italy and Argentina).

The first quarter-final paired New Zealand with Scotland and the contest turned into a one-sided affair with the All Blacks scoring two tries (Alan Whetton and John Gallagher) to Scotland's none. Grant Fox scored six penalties and two conversions while Scotland's Gavin Hastings could only score one penalty as they exited the competition by a 30-3 margin.

The second match saw a closer-fought contest between France and Fiji but the European side were too strong for the islanders from the South Pacific and recorded a 31-16 victory with tries from Laurent Rodriguez (2), Patrice Lagisquet and Alain Lorieux together with Guy Laporte's successful kicks (three conversions, two penalties and one drop goal). Fiji put in a good performance and responded with two tries of their own from Manasa Qoro and Jimi Damu while Severo Koroduadua Waqanibau scored one conversion and two penalties.

The third quarter-final paired Australia and Ireland but, although the Irish put up a valiant fight, the Wallabies were too strong for them and ran out 33-15 winners. Michael Kiernan proved to be Ireland's main point scorer with one try – Hugh MacNeill crossed the line for their other touchdown – two conversions and a penalty. In contrast, the Australians claimed four tries

(Matt Burke 2, Andrew McIntyre and Brian Smith), with Michael Lynagh scoring four conversions and three penalties.

In the last quarter-final, arch-rivals Wales and England were pitted together. With neither side enjoying success on the domestic front, it proved an interesting battle but it was the Red Dragons who emerged victorious. Tries by John Devereux, Robert Jones and Gareth Roberts, coupled with two Paul Thorburn conversions gave Wales a commanding 16-3 victory. England could only manage a consolation penalty from Jon Webb.

New Zealand effortlessly dispatched Wales' semi-final challenge with tries from John Kirwan (2), Wayne Shelford (2), Mark Brooke-Cowden, John Drake, Joe Stanley and Alan Whetton. With Grant Fox converting seven of those tries and adding a penalty, New Zealand quickly racked up a 49-6 triumph. Wales' points came from a John Devereux try, converted by Paul Thorburn.

In the other semi-final, pre-tournament favourites Australia took on reigning Five Nations Grand Slam holders France. The pattern of the game quickly settled, with the co-hosts taking the lead and France pegging them back a notch or two. Playing attractive rugby, the Wallabies took the lead three times and each time the French replied in kind. Australia recorded two tries courtesy of David Campese and David Cody, only for the French trio of Alain Lorieux, Philippe Sella and Patrice Lagisquet to cross the goal-line themselves.

Michael Lynagh had several chances to extend the Wallabies' lead but missed what would turn out to be vital penalty kicks. He nevertheless ended the game with 16 points from three penalties, two conversions and a drop goal. His counterpart on the French team was Didier Camberabero, who had kicked three conversions and two penalties as the game entered the latter stages.

The French were awarded another penalty which Camberabero slotted through the posts to level the match at 24-24 and extra-time loomed. But France had other ideas and the move that brought the winning try started deep in their own half. With the ball dancing from player to player, it had passed through the hands of 11 players before it reached Serge Blanco, who made no mistake and threw off the challenge of Tom Lawton to charge to the line. Camberabero succeeded with the conversion to give France a famous 30-24 victory and a place in the final.

Wales took advantage of a shell-shocked Australia to win the third-place play-off by 22-1 while New Zealand showed their world-beating qualities by demolishing France 29-9 in the final.

SCOTLAND BEAT ENGLAND IN GRAND SLAM DECIDER
1990

There are few things that can rile a Scotsman more than an over-confident Englishman so it was no surprise that Scotland had a bee in their bonnet with reported stories of T-shirts and ties bearing the proclamation "England Grand Slam 1990" being sold in the streets of Edinburgh before the final game of that season's Five Nations championship.

France had dominated the tournament in the 1980s, winning six titles (although they shared three with Ireland, Scotland and Wales) and three Grand Slams. They got their campaign off to a winning start with a 29-19 victory over Wales in Cardiff Arms Park with tries from Didier Camberabero, Jean-Baptiste Lafond, Laurent Rodriguez, Philippe Sella and Patrice Lagisquet. The same weekend, England were trouncing their Irish counterparts 23-0 at Twickenham. Tries from David Egerton, Rory Underwood, Jerry Guscott and Jeff Probyn announced their intention to reclaim their title.

The next matchday saw Scotland kickstart their campaign with a 13-10 victory at Lansdowne Road. Trailing to Ireland 7-0 from a Michael Kiernan try and a John Fitzgerald penalty at half-time, it was Scottish number 8 Derek White who revitalised his team with two tries after the interval. Craig Chalmers converted one and scored a penalty to give Scotland a winning start. England continued as they had started, with a convincing 26-7 triumph in Paris. Underwood and Guscott were again on the scoresheet while captain Will Carling scored his country's third try. Simon Hodgkinson converted one and successfully kicked four penalties to complete England's scoring.

Scotland's next opponents were defending champions France, already smarting from the defeat at the hands of English, and they would fare no better at Murrayfield. Gavin Hastings kicked a penalty to register the only score of the first half, but the dismissal of flanker Alain Carminati saw the French reduced to 14 players and Scotland took full advantage. Finlay Calder carried the ball over the French goal-line for the Scot's first try, a feat which Iwan Tukalo emulated, while Chalmers converted both tries and scored two penalties.

SCOTLAND BEAT ENGLAND IN GRAND SLAM DECIDER

GREATEST MOMENTS OF RUGBY

England continued their assault on the title with a 34-6 thrashing of an inept Wales side. Rory Underwood scored a brace of tries, while Carling and Richard Hill added one apiece. Hodgkinson's three conversions and four penalties gave him a tally of 18 points for that game while Wales could only manage a Phil Davies try that was converted by Paul Thorburn.

France regained some national pride when they entertained Ireland on 3 March in their final match of the campaign. Tries from Franck Mesnel (2) and Lagisquet and 19 points from the boot of Camberabero (five penalties and two conversions) outscored Kiernan's four penalties to give them a 31-12 victory. In the other match that day, Scotland were aiming to keep their Grand Slam hopes alive with a visit to Cardiff Arms Park. The two teams managed one try apiece – Arthur Jones scoring for the home side and Damien Cronin for the visitors – so it all came down to the battle of the kickers. Chalmers emerged victorious in that mini encounter, scoring three penalties to Thorburn's one plus conversion.

With television pictures of the England captain psyching his team up by telling them that they were better than Scotland, the scene was set for a classic Calcutta Cup match at Murrayfield. Scotland emerged behind captain David Sole with the roar of the crowd in their ears and sang "Flower Of Scotland" for the first time at an international match instead of the national anthem.

Scotland's tactics were simple, close down the English players so that they did not have a chance to get into their rhythm and pressurise them into making mistakes or giving away needless penalties. Their gameplan worked and, within the first 10 minutes, Chalmers had kicked the home side into a 6-0 lead after penalties were awarded against Dooley for offending in a ruck and Probyn for stamping. England reduced the deficit minutes later when Guscott scored his country's first try at Murrayfield for 10 years but Chalmers recorded a third penalty to send Scotland in 9-4 ahead at the break.

When the next score came after the interval, it sent the home crowd wild. When the ball was released from the scrum, Gavin Hastings chipped it forwards for Tony Stanger to catch and dive over the line. Although Hodgkinson added another three points to the visitors' score, he would struggle with the exceptionally strong wind all afternoon and missed several kicks that would have sent the Grand Slam across the border instead.

In the final game of the campaign, Ireland and Wales battled it out at the other end of the table to avoid the wooden spoon. Ireland succeeded and registered their only points of the tournament with a 14-8 victory at Lansdowne Road.

ENGLAND 25-22 AUSTRALIA, WORLD CUP QUARTER-FINAL 1995

The third World Cup, in 1995, saw every match being held in the same country for the first time in the competition's history (Australia and New Zealand having co-hosted the first tournament and Europe's Five Nations' members staging the 1991 event). As had happened four years previously, the eight quarter-finalists from the previous tournament gained automatic entry into the 1995 World Cup along with South Africa as hosts.

The remaining seven slots were fought for in regional qualifiers, a new experience for Wales who had failed to progress past the group stages after their shock opening match defeat against Western Samoa in Cardiff.

The competition was still organised in the same format with four groups of four nations playing each other once with the top two teams in each group going through to the knockout stage. The only difference in the tournament itself was that tries were now worth five points.

The opening match saw hosts South Africa take on defending champions Australia in Cape Town and the Springboks registered their first ever World Cup victory in style. Pieter Hendricks and Joel Stransky led the charge with one try apiece with the latter player also kicking a further 17 points. Australia replied with two tries of their own from Phil Kearns and Michael Lynagh but went down 18-27.

The Wallabies did, however, record wins in their remaining two group matches to secure their place in the quarter-finals. Canada were dispatched 27-11, with Michael Lynagh, Tabua Tamanivalu and Joe Roff all scoring tries. Lynagh also added three conversions and two penalties to secure the victory. The Canadians, on the other hand, managed one try by Alan Charron and two penalties from the boot of Gareth Rees.

There was a more convincing scoreline in their final group match, a 42-3 thumping of Romania. The Wallabies scored five tries – Damian Smith, David Wilson, Joe Roff, Michael Foley and Matt Burke – while John Eales took over the kicking duties and racked up 17 points with four conversions and three penalties.

Their quarter-final opponents England, meanwhile, had come through the group stage with a 100% record, winning all three of their matches. In their opening game in Durban against Argentina, they were outscored in tries by two to nil with Lisandro Arbizu and Patricio Moriega touching down for the South Americans. Luckily for England, Rob Andrew scored 24 points, kicking six penalties and two drop goals.

ENGLAND 25-22 AUSTRALIA, WORLD CUP QUARTER-FINAL

GREATEST MOMENTS OF RUGBY

Their second game pitted them against European rivals Italy and in a close-fought encounter the Five Nations' Grand Slam holders edged out the Azzurri by 27-20. Brothers Rory and Tony Underwood scored a try apiece with Rob Andrew kicking the remaining 17 points. In reply, Italy scored two tries from Massimo Cuttitta and Paolo Vaccari with Diego Dominguez registering two penalties and two conversions.

Western Samoa were beaten 44-22 in the final group game, with Rory Underwood (2) and Neil Back providing England's tries. Jon Callard took over the kicking duties and Mike Catt scored a drop goal to set up a quarter-final clash in Cape Town with the current World Cup holders Australia.

The English pack started well and dominated their opposing numbers in the first half. Michael Lynagh opened the scoring with a penalty before Rob Andrew slotted two of his own through the posts to make it 6-3 but a rare Australian mistake gave the English backs the opportunity to launch a counter-attack. Andrew pounced on a Lynagh fumble and fed Jerry Guscott who quickly passed to Will Carling. As Tony Underwood sped up on his right shoulder, the England captain released the winger who headed for the corner. Damian Smith made a valiant attempt to catch Underwood but was unsuccessful and Andrew converted the try. Lynagh was successful with another penalty and England took a 13-6 lead into half-time.

Australia scored first as the second half got under way when Lynagh launched a huge up and under towards England's goal-line. As Mike Catt and Underwood waited underneath it, Damian Smith jumped between them and caught the ball before rolling over the tryline. Lynagh's conversion levelled the scores at 13-13. The two fly-halves traded penalties until the score was 22-22 and the game went into extra-time.

England won a line-out part way into the Australian half when Martin Bayfield took a catch and the forwards pushed towards the tryline. As the ball came out, Dewi Morris passed to Andrew who only had one thing on his mind. With his head down, Andrew unleashed a 45-yard drop-kick that sailed through the uprights to win this classic encounter for England.

Unfortunately for England, they came up against eventual winners New Zealand and Jonah Lomu in the semi-finals where they lost 45-29. In the third-place play-off, they were unable to recreate their try-scoring magic and lost 19-9 to France.

SOUTH AFRICA BEAT NEW ZEALAND IN FINAL 1995

Previously boycotted from international sporting events, South Africa were participating in their first World Cup since the abolition of Apartheid on 27 April 1994, now a public holiday in that country named Freedom Day. Indeed, such was the transformation in South Africa that they were actually hosting the 1995 World Cup although only one black player – Chester Williams – would play any part in their games. But, with his speed and ability, it was obvious that Williams had been included in the team on his own merits rather than to appease critics.

As happens with many sporting spectaculars, many of the stadiums that were due to stage the matches were upgraded, with the biggest four – Ellis Park (Johannesburg), Loftus Versfeld (Pretoria), Newlands (Cape Town) and Kings Park Stadium (Durban) – being chosen to host the knockout stages. The tournament did not go without a hitch, however, as the weather played a hand in proceedings. Few will forget the sight of people with brooms sweeping water from the pitch after a torrential downpour.

The opening match saw South Africa face Australia in Cape Town and tries from Pieter Hendricks and Joel Stransky helped the Springboks to record their first ever World Cup victory. Australia replied with two tries from Phil Kearns and Michael Lynagh. So it was down to the fly-halves and Stransky outscored Lynagh by 17 points to eight to give the Springboks a 27-18 win.

South Africa faced Romania in their next game and eased to a 21-8 victory with two tries from Adriaan Richter. Gavin Johnson scored three penalties and a conversion to complete the scoring for the host nation. In reply, Romania's Andrei Guranescu scored a try and Ilie Ivancuic a penalty. The Springboks' third tie was against Canada and they scored 20 points without reply to book their place in the quarter-finals. Richter again crossed the line twice, with Stransky converting both tries and adding two penalties.

New Zealand meanwhile were cruising through their group, racking up a massive points total along the way. Ireland were dispatched 43-19 with the All Blacks scoring five tries including two from Maori sensation Jonah Lomu. Wales were the next opponents but they could not stop the

southern hemisphere side running a victorious 34-9 scoreline. Although New Zealand were restricted to three times this time out, Andrew Mehrtens kicked 19 points to hand the Welsh their first defeat of the tournament. This was followed by a game that rewrote the record books. New Zealand scored a massive 21 tries against Japan in a slaughtering 145-17 performance. Marc Ellis registered the most number of tries in a game with six while Simon Culhane kicked a record 20 conversions.

In the quarter-finals, South Africa breezed past Western Samoa 42-14 while the All Blacks had to work a bit harder to defeat Scotland 48-30. The semi-finals saw New Zealand again register a high-scoring win, this time 45-29 over England, with Lomu scoring four tries. South Africa overcame France by 19-15 to set up a showpiece final meeting in Johannesburg.

While the final did not produce any tries, it was an intriguing contest that was ultimately decided by how accurate the kicking was of each country's fly-half. The first half saw Joel Stransky edge in front with two penalties and a drop goal while Andrew Mehrtens could only score two penalties as South Africa went into the interval 9-6 ahead.

The second half resulted in much of the same, with Mehrtens levelling the scores up through another penalty. Both fly-halves scored another penalty to make the final score 12-12 and send the match into extra-time. Neither side could add another score in the first half of added time and all eyes were on the clock as it wound down towards the end of the allotted time. Luckily for the home nation, Stransky managed to secure the title with his second drop goal of the game and South Africa won 15-12.

After the match it was left to Nelson Mandela to present the trophy to the winning captain. Mandela – who had been imprisoned for 27 years under Apartheid and held for the majority of that time on the notorious Robben Island – became Prime Minister the previous year when his ANC Party had been elected to power. He would hold this post until 1999.

Mandela, in what was seen as a move to reconcile black and white South Africans, had issued a rallying cry for the whole country to get behind the Springboks who – buoyed by the nation's support – duly delivered the title. On 24 June 1995, Nelson Mandela – wearing a Springbok jersey – presented the William Webb Ellis Cup to South African captain Francois Pienaar in front of a capacity crowd at Johannesburg's Ellis Park Stadium.

BATH, FIRST ENGLISH WIN- NERS OF THE HEINEKEN CUP 1998

It was more than fitting for Bath Rugby Football Club to become the first British winners of the Heineken Cup in 1997-98. Founded more than 140 years ago, in 1865, Bath have a long history of success both as an amateur side and a professional outfit. Many have labelled them the most "professional" amateur side before the big changes of the 1990s.

Bath enjoyed great success in the 1980s, winning the John Player Special and Pilkington Cups – the forerunners of today's EDF Energy Cup – 10 times between 1984 and 1996. They also won the Premier League six times in eight years and on four of those occasions completed the Double, Leicester achieved this feat in 2007. They made history in May 1996 by playing Wigan Rugby League Football Club at their own game – losing 82-6 – and then emerging victorious under Union rules (44-19) a fortnight later.

Proposed by the Five Nations Committee, the Heineken Cup – known as the H Cup in France due to alcohol advertising restrictions – was launched in 1995 to encourage more international competition between the professional clubs. The inaugural competition did not include English and Scottish teams, however, because the new competition could not be fitted into their already hectic fixture schedule.

Having previously consisted of group games with the teams meeting just once prior to the knockout stage, the 1997-98 tournament saw the introduction of teams meeting on a home and away basis in the pool games. The five pools of four sides guaranteed each team a minimum of six games and the three quarter-final play-off matches all added up to a 70-match tournament.

Bath's route to the final saw them overcome Pontypridd (21-15 and 23-10), The Borders (31-17 and 27-23) and Brive (27-25 but the Rec outfit lost the return 12-29) in the pool matches before disposing of Cardiff Blues (32-21) and Pau (20-14) in the knockout stages. The quarter-finals saw Brive ease past London Wasps before a hard-fought encounter with countrymen Toulouse.

The build-up to the final could not have been more unsettling for Bath. A group of 12 English clubs had already reached the decision to withdraw from the following season's competition in an

argument over fixture scheduling and money while Jonathan Callard was forced to take his practice kicking session at Stade Lescure, a football stadium without any rugby posts! Add to that Phil de Glanville's last-minute decision to play despite his wife being in hospital after complications in childbirth and it makes Bath's achievement even more remarkable.

So it was that Bath took on defending champions Brive – who had conquered Leicester Tigers 28-9 the previous year in Cardiff – in Bordeaux's Stade Lescure and for most of the match it looked like the Frenchmen could retain their title. Brive were in front at half-time by five Christophe Lamaison penalties to Callard's two to give the French side a 15-6 lead.

But things were about to change early in the second half: Brive were laying an all-out onslaught on the Bath try-line and it seemed only a matter of time before they would score a well-deserved try. Bath, however, were not ready to cave in and successfully defended seven attempted tries in quick succession before being awarded a welcome penalty and the opportunity to relieve the pressure. "We could have conceded a try," admitted Callard, "but our pack were awesome."

So the tide had turned and it was Bath's opportunity to put the Brive players under the cosh. Callard turned the occasion into a one-man scoring event, adding a try, conversion and another penalty to take his – and Bath's – tally to 16. Brive, meanwhile, had added another three points through Alain Penaud's 65th-minute drop goal.

With the clock ticking down, it wasn't until 80 seconds into injury-time that Callard had the final say, with his fourth penalty giving Bath a 19-18 lead. Not that that was the end of the match as the Frenchmen could have nicked it just at the end. Lamaison watched his final penalty kick of the game go wide of the post while fly-half Lisandro Arbizu could also have deflated the Bath faithful had his drop goal effort been on target. As it was, Bath held on for a well-deserved victory and came home to a heroes' welcome.

Bath (who, sticking by the boycott, were unable to defend their title the following year) have suffered more than most clubs in the professional era, being deprived of a head coach who departed to take control of the England team – Jack Rowell in 1995 – and narrowly avoiding a merger with Bristol and relegation in 2002-03. But 31 January 1998 will forever live on in the memories of the dedicated fans who trust that further glory is just around the corner.

NEWCASTLE, FIRST "PRO-FESSIONAL" LEAGUE CHAMPIONS 1998

The first professional Rugby Union club in England, Newcastle Falcons, found a willing benefactor in local businessman Sir John Hall who was determined to put Newcastle on the sporting map. As well as taking control of the Falcons, Hall bought controlling interests in Newcastle United Football Club, Newcastle Eagles basketball team and Newcastle Wasps – currently renamed the Vipers – ice hockey team.

The origins of the club date back to 1877 when a group of Durham School old boys founded the Gosforth Club. They chose a strip of green and white hoops but it wasn't until the late 1970s that the club enjoyed success on a national scale. Gosforth won the John Player Cup in 1976 and 1977 and were runners-up in 1981 but it was the arrival of Hall who (just as he did at Newcastle United) made the Newcastle club – they changed their name to Newcastle Gosforth in 1990 – a force to be feared.

It was Hall who persuaded former England World Cup hero Rob Andrew to take on the position of director of rugby in 1996 and the success story was about to begin. Andrew is credited with discovering the talents of a certain Jonny Wilkinson who made his breakthrough into the Newcastle side during the 1997-98 season. By the following season, he had already broken into the international side.

Another name change arrived in time for the 1996-97 with the monicker Falcons replacing Gosforth and a new strip of black and white was installed. That season saw the club finish second in the Courage National Division Two, one point behind Richmond. They played West Hartlepool in the play-off and triumphed to secure a place in the top flight.

The financial set-up of clubs in the Premiership is not at all like that of a Premiership football club. While the football club depends on the backing of the owner to pay players etc, clubs in the Guinness Premiership were allocated £2 million – this was raised to £2.25 million in 2004-05 – to pay their players' seasonal wage bill. The clubs are also paid £30,000 per England player per year by the RFU on the understanding that they will release their players for international duty.

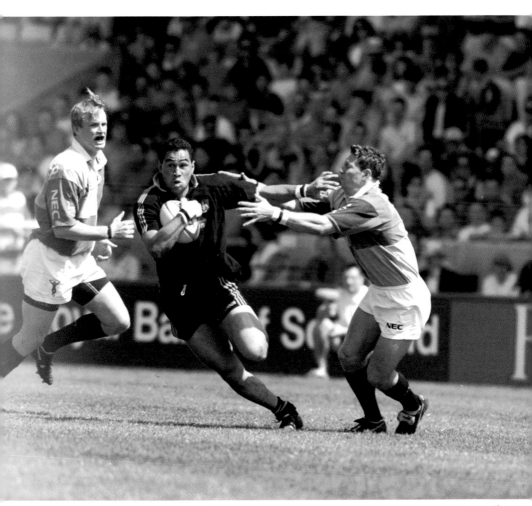

GREATEST MOMENTS OF RUGBY

Newcastle Falcons' inaugural match in the Guinness Premiership saw them visit Bath's Recreation Ground on 23 August 1997 where they emerged 20-13 victors. They followed up this success with three matches in October that saw them add another six points to their tally. Northampton Saints and Richmond were beaten at Kingston Park (37-12 and 18-12 respectively) while Sale Sharks were disposed of 33-26 in that month's only away league fixture.

The following month saw the Falcons make the journey to face London Irish where they triumphed 35-19 while December saw three fixtures fulfilled. Gloucester were the only visitors to Kingston Park but left empty-handed after a 27-37 defeat. The week between Christmas and New Year saw the Falcons on the road again with Bristol Shoguns thrashed 50-8 and Leicester Tigers putting up more of a fight but still ending up losing 19-25.

January 1998 saw the return matches with London Irish and Northampton Saints. In the first match, the Irish were dismissed 46-13 at Kingston Park while the last day of the month saw the Falcons travel to Franklin's Gardens where they managed to ease past Northampton by 21-17. It looked as if the financial investments made by Sir John Hall were going to pay dividends as the season was now entering February and the Falcons had yet to be beaten.

Their next two games saw them overcome the challenges of NEC Harlequins (43-15) and Sale Sharks (23-18) before they suffered their first setback of the campaign with a 17-30 reverse at Richmond. Their closest rivals in the league table were Saracens who had lost just once – 21-22 against Leicester Tigers – so the Falcons knew they could not afford to be complacent and that they needed to get back to winning ways.

They did just that with a 30-25 victory over Saracens at Kingston Park before beating defending champions London Wasps 20-13 and Gloucester. Falcons then narrowly lost against Saracens (10-12) and Wasps (17-18) before finishing their season with four straight wins against Bristol Shoguns (43-18), Leicester Tigers (27-10), Bath (20-15) and NEC Harlequins (44-20) to secure the 1997-98 Guinness Premiership title. Luckily, Saracens had also endured a couple of setbacks – losing 15-38 to Gloucester and drawing 10-10 with Leicester Tigers – and would finish the season one point behind Newcastle.

Unfortunately for Falcons fans, the success of this season would prove to be a false dawn as Newcastle failed to build upon the success of their 1997-98 season. Indeed, it would be another six years before Newcastle found themselves on top of the Guinness Premiership, when they defeated NEC Harlequins 22-21 in September 2004.

NEWCASTLE FIRST "PROFESSIONAL" LEAGUE CHAMPIONS 51

WALES BEAT SOUTH AFRICA AT THE MILLENNIUM STADIUM 1999

There were tears in the eyes of many Welsh rugby fans when the old Cardiff Arms Park was demolished in 1997. It had been the home to the national side for more years than most would care to remember, had seen some wonderful triumphs and the turf had been graced by players such as Barry John, Phil Bennett, Gareth Edwards, JPR Williams, Rob Howley, Jonathan Davies and Neil Jenkins.

The site – behind the Cardiff Arms Hotel – was originally a meadow owned by the Marquess of Bute, who stipulated that it should only be used for recreational purposes. It was sold to Cardiff Athletic Club and the Welsh Rugby Union in 1922 but was bombed by the Luftwaffe in 1941.

The new Millennium Stadium was completed at a cost of £126 million – a remarkably low budget bearing in mind the spiralling cost of rebuilding Wembley rose to around £800 million – including £46 million in funds from the National Lottery. The stadium, completed in time to host the 1999 World Cup, has an all-seater capacity of 74,500 but the first game to be played there saw Wales take on world champions South Africa on 26 June 1999.

As the finishing touches were still being completed, there were only 27,683 who can claim that they were actually there when Wales beat the Springboks for the first time in the history of the fixture. Wales lost the first match 11-0 in February 1906 and the closest they had ever come to beating South Africa was a 6-6 draw at Cardiff Arms Park in January 1970.

This was the 13th meeting between the two nations and it would prove unlucky for South Africa. In previous encounters, the Springboks had emerged victorious on 11 occasions, inflicting some heavy and, at times, embarrassing defeats on the Red Dragons. Few can forget the 40-11 thrashing in September 1995 or the 96-13 mauling in June 1998 (both of these games took place in South Africa). But passions and patriotism were running high in June 1999 as Wales took to the field for the first time in their new home.

Wales started well and a Peter Rogers thrust won a penalty after South Africa handled in the ruck. Neil Jenkins made no mistake with the kick to score the first points at the new stadium. It wasn't

long before South Africa were level with Braam van Straaten successfully kicking a penalty after Scott Quinnell had been found guilty of going over the top of a ruck.

The Springboks gave away another needless penalty minutes later when Robbie Kempson was penalised for going over the top after Shane Howarth had been felled. As usual, Neil Jenkins's kick gave his side another three points and a 6-3 lead. He had a chance to extend Wales' lead minutes later after an infringement on Chris Wyatt at a line-out. Not needing to see that the kick was successful, Jenkins turned to run back to his half and the home side now had a six-point advantage.

South Africa reduced the deficit to three points after a period where Wales found it difficult to gain territory with the southern hemisphere side ensuring that ferocious tackles were made before Wales could have a chance to put together some coherent passing. But South Africa were then guilty of collapsing a scrum but the attending fans saw a rare Jenkins miss which kept the score at 9-6. It wasn't long before he had a chance to redeem himself after the visitors again played the ball on the ground in a ruck, however, and this time he made no mistake to take his side to 12-6. There was still enough time before the interval for Mark Taylor to score a spectacular try that sent the stadium wild after Colin Charvis had gathered the loose ball at a line-out. Jenkins converted to set up a half-time score of 19-6.

The second half saw South Africa come out determined to bring parity to the game and it wasn't long before Werner Swanepoel crossed the line for an unconverted try. Determined defending saw Wales prevent South Africa from adding to their tally until Gaffie du Toit added another penalty. A further try from Gareth Thomas plus another five points from the boot of Jenkins gave the Welsh a well-deserved 29-19 victory over the World Champions despite a try from Percy Montgomery.

The Millennium Stadium may have been overtaken as the largest in the UK by the redeveloped Twickenham and the newly-opened Wembley Stadium, but the name of Cardiff Arms Park has not been consigned to the history books. Cardiff Rugby Club still uses the name for its own ground on the site of the Millennium Stadium and the Arms Park Choir can still be heard singing traditional songs and the national anthem in the local pubs whenever Wales are playing.

FRANCE 43-31 NEW ZEALAND, WORLD CUP SEMI-FINAL 1999

New Zealand were again favourites to lift the William Webb Ellis Trophy when the fourth World Cup was contested in 1999. Officially hosted by Wales – although matches were also staged in France, England, Scotland and Ireland – this tournament saw a change in the qualification rules with only the holders, runners-up and third-placed team from four years earlier gaining an automatic entry.

In previous tournaments, the eight quarter-finalists did not have to go through the qualification process. This time round, the likes of England, Australia, Scotland and Ireland would have to fight it out with 61 other nations for the remaining 16 places. This competition saw the 20 teams divided into five groups of four with a quarter-final play-off round between the five group runners-up and the best third-placed team before the knockout stages began in earnest.

The tournament – which had grown to be the third largest international sporting event in the world behind the Olympics and the FIFA World Cup – saw Wales register a 23-18 victory over Argentina on the opening day. Tries from Colin Charvis and Mark Taylor plus 13 points from the boot of their prolific kicker Neil Jenkins – who would finish the tournament as the world's leading point scorer in international rugby with 941 – were enough to see off Gonzalo Quesada's six penalties. They went on to beat Japan 64-15 with eight tries being scored, and qualified for the quarter-finals as group winners despite losing their last pool game against Western Samoa (31-38).

Defending champions South Africa breezed through their group with impressive victories against Scotland (46-29), Spain (47-3) and Uruguay (39-3) while their opponents in the 1995 final, New Zealand, were drawn in the same group as England. The All Blacks won all three of their group games – against Tonga (45-9), England (30-16) and Italy (101-3) – with Jonah Lomu scoring five tries. This would be the tournament where he cemented his reputation as one of the world's best players. England enjoyed comfortable victories over Italy (67-7) and Tonga (101-10) to claim their place in the quarter-final play-offs.

France and Australia were the two other teams who won all three of their group matches. France triumphed over Canada (33-20), Namibia (47-13) and Fiji (28-19) while the Wallabies eased

through qualification with wins against Romania (57-9), Ireland (23-3) and the United States (55-19). The quarter-finals saw relatively comfortable wins for Australia (24-9 against Wales), South Africa (44-21 against England), France (47-26 against Argentina) and New Zealand (30-18 over Scotland).

GREATEST MOMENTS OF RUGBY

Both semi-finals were held at Twickenham and Australia triumphed over South Africa in the first match. There were no tries scored as Matthew Burke kicked eight penalties to add to Stephen Larkham's drop goal for the Wallabies while all the Springboks' points came from the boot of Jan Hendrik de Beer. But what the first semi-final lacked in free-flowing rugby, the second more than made up for in excitement and spectacular tries.

It was the underdogs France who registered the first try with Christophe Lamaison – who was only in the side because of an injury to Thomas Castaignede – after a fantastic break by Christian Dominici but the All Blacks were soon in front and it was courtesy of the human bulldozer Jonah Lomu. At 6′ 5″ and 18 stone, the Tongan-born winger proved unstoppable for many opponents and he was soon on the scoresheet against the French, crossing the line for two tries. Andrew Mehrtens converted one of these tries and added four penalties to give New Zealand a healthy 24-10 lead.

But that's when it all started to go wrong for the All Blacks as Lamaison scored two drop goals and two penalties to reduce the deficit to just two points. A stunned crowd watched as New Zealand's experienced team began to panic rather than continue playing constructive rugby as they had been.

France then scored three tries – Dominici, Richard Douorthe and Philippe Bernat-Salles – without reply, all of which were converted by Lamaison to turn the tide and stretch their lead to 43-24. Although the All Blacks did score another converted try (Jeff Wilson), their dream was over and France had completed an amazing comeback to record an historic 43-31 victory.

Sadly it seemed that France had expended all their energy and skill in this match because when they faced Australia in the final at the Millennium Stadium they were unrecognisable from the side that had tortured the All Blacks. While Lamaison was again on the scoresheet with four penalties, they were the only points the Cockerels managed and the Wallabies ran up a total of 35 points with tries from Ben Tune and Owen Finegan adding to Burke's seven penalties and two conversions.

Such was the excitement over Australia's second world title that parades were held in Sydney, Melbourne and Brisbane where the team were presented with the keys to each city. There was a ticker-tape procession in Sydney attended by tens of thousands of fans.

...AND ITALY MAKE IT SIX...
2000

The Five Nations underwent a name change in 2000 as the competition was expanded to include a sixth country: Italy. It was the first change in format since 1947, when France were readmitted after the Second World War following their ejection from the tournament in 1931 amid allegations of non-professionalism and violence on the pitch.

Rugby had been introduced to the Italians at the end of the 19th century but the *Federazione Italiana Rugby* (FIR) did not come into being until 1928 when it emerged from an earlier Propaganda Committee. The first national championship took place the following year along with the first international, a 0-9 defeat against Spain. They played France for the first time in 1937 that resulted in a 43-5 victory for the French (the winners of this fixture have, from February 2007, been awarded the Giuseppe Garibaldi Trophy). The Italians began pressuring the organisers of the Five Nations to let them take part in the 1980s but it was not until 2000 that they were successful. By then, Italy had taken part in four World Cups.

The Azzurri's first game in the Six Nations was when Scotland visited Rome for the opening round of matches in February 2000 and there would not have been many bookmakers who would have given Italy much chance of registering an upset. Defending champions and World Cup quarter-finalists Scotland began the game as expected, dominating the first 20 minutes. But one of the side's most potent attacking threats, captain John Leslie, had to limp off with little more than 10 minutes of the game gone so the Scots' rhythm was not running smoothly. They did, however, keep pounding at the Italian defence to no avail. Kenny Logan missed a couple of penalties before Gregor Townsend notched the first points with a drop goal.

It wasn't long before the Italians responded, with Diego Dominguez successfully converting two penalties but Scotland registered the first try of the game. In a comedy of errors, Townsend recovered from a disastrous pass to flip the ball to Glenn Metcalfe who was tackled near the line by Alessandro Troncon. As he fell, Metcalfe's foot connected with the ball kicking it forward for Gordon Bulloch to touch down. Logan added the two points from the conversion – his only

successful kick of the game – before Dominguez scored two more penalties to send the Italians into the interval with a 12-10 lead.

The second half continued in the same fashion, with Dominguez adding two more penalties and three drop goals before Giampiero De Carli scored Italy's first Six Nations try. Scotland replied with a Martin Leslie try that was converted by Townsend, who also scored a penalty to give a final score of Italy 34 Scotland 20.

The result may have shocked most people, but not everyone had been anticipating doom and gloom. "I thought if we were going to win a match it was going to be the first one," admitted Italy coach Brad Johnstone. "Everybody expected us to be useless. I feel sorry for the Scots because they hit us first."

Italy's first away match produced a very different result to their inaugural home match when they came up against a Wales side still smarting from their opening day 3-36 defeat at home to France. The Red Dragons cruised to a 47-16 victory with tries from Shane Howarth, Scott Quinnell, Allan Bateman and Shane Williams.

Wales, however, later became entangled in the "Grannygate" scandal when it was discovered that New Zealanders Shane Howarth and Brett Sinkinson had played despite being ineligible. The WRU had made only a cursory check of their ancestry, and the pair were suspended from international rugby.

The Azzurri suffered their biggest defeat of the campaign when they headed to Ireland in March. Trailing 33-0 at half-time at Lansdowne Road, Ireland continued piling on the misery after the interval to finish with a 60-13 victory. They scored six tries with Shane Horgan getting two while Keith Wood, Girvan Dempsey, Kieron Dawson and Brian O'Driscoll each registered one apiece.

England were the next visitors to Rome's Stadio Flaminio and they inflicted another on the Italians en route to the Six Nations title. Three tries by Austin Healey and tries apiece from Matt Dawson and Ben Cohen ensured England's fourth victory of the campaign while Italy's Cristian Stoica and Luca Martin each touched down. In their final match of the tournament, Italy visited France and put up an admirable performance despite losing 31-42 with tries from Troncon (2), Martin and Nicola Mazzucato.

Elsewhere, Scotland ruined England's Grand Slam dream yet again with a 19-13 victory at Murrayfield that earned them their only points of the campaign and handed the wooden spoon to Italy. France, Ireland and Wales all finished two points behind England, having lost one more game.

ENGLAND WIN SIX NATIONS WITH RECORD SCORING 2001

The 2001 Six Nations championship will be remembered for several reasons. First, the outbreak of foot and mouth disease which disrupted the tournament and forced Ireland to play their last three matches seven months later after the government had control of the epidemic that decimated livestock herds across the UK.

Second, for the cavalier way in which England sauntered to massive wins against Wales, Italy, Scotland and France, and third because they blew their chance of a Grand Slam for the third time in three years. In 1999, Wales – playing their home games at Wembley Stadium while construction of the Millennium Stadium was ongoing – fought their way to a thrilling 32-31 victory over England on the last day of the campaign. As mentioned previously in this book, Scotland repeated that feat with a 19-13 win at Murrayfield in 2000 while this year would be Ireland's turn.

The tournament began well for Ireland in February who – having met the Pope before the games – recorded a 41-22 triumph over Italy in Rome. Three tries from Rob Henderson, together with one apiece from Ronan O'Gara and Shane Horgan, set the Irish on the road to victory. The Italians managed three tries in reply, from Corrado Pilat, Carlo Checchinato and Mauro Bergamasco.

The other opening day fixtures saw England trounce Wales by 44-15 and France beat Scotland 16-6. The tension in the Millennium Stadium was boosted by the fact that Wales coach Graham Henry had been chosen ahead of Clive Woodward to take the Lions on tour and had suggested that the England players would play well in order to impress him when he selected his squad. The difference in class was evident as England inflicted Wales' heaviest-ever defeat in Cardiff with six tries being scored by Will Greenwood (3), Matt Dawson (2) and Ben Cohen. One small consolation for the Welsh was that Neil Jenkins' conversion and penalty saw him become the first player to break the 1,000-point barrier.

The second weekend saw Scotland and Wales play out a 28-28 draw at Murrayfield while Ireland edged to a 22-15 victory over France at Lansdowne Road. England, meanwhile, were terrorising Italy at Twickenham and racking up 10 tries in the process.

GREATEST MOMENTS OF RUGBY

The first half saw the Italians score two tries – Denis Dallan and Carlo Checchinato – with full-back Andrea Scanavacca adding 13 points with two conversions and three penalties. England responded with two tries from Austin Healey, one from Cohen and seven successful kicks from Jonny Wilkinson to take a 33-23 lead into the half-time interval. Unfortunately for the Azzurri, they would be unable to add to their first-half score as they crashed to a thunderous 80-23 defeat. Second-half tries from Cohen, Lawrence Dallaglio, Iain Balshaw (2), Wilkinson, Mark Regan, Joe Worsley and Greenwood completed the rout.

England's next game saw them up against Scotland at Twickenham and about to inflict a record defeat on another neighbour. After a minute's silence in memory of the victims of the recent Selby rail crash, Dallaglio breached the Scottish defence after seven minutes to open the floodgates before Duncan Hodge registered Scotland's only score with a penalty. Richard Hill and Dallaglio (again) added further tries before half-time to send England in with a 22-3 lead. Second-half touchdowns from Balshaw (2) and Greenwood gave England a record 43-3 Calcutta Cup win. With three games under their belt, England had already scored 22 tries…more than any other team had ever managed in a complete campaign.

In the other games, Italy put in a respectable performance and lost 19-30 to France. The following set of games saw England resting as they should have been playing Ireland but Scotland narrowly edged past Italy 23-19 while Wales restored some national pride with an exciting 43-35 victory in Paris.

The French were even more unlucky next time out as they ended up on the wrong end of a 48-19 scoreline at Twickenham. A stunning display by the home team saw another six tries scored while Wilkinson's 18-point tally took him past Rob Andrews' record. In the other fixture, Wales could not find the consistency they enjoyed in Paris but still recorded a 33-23 victory over Italy in Rome before the enforced five-month break in the championship.

The first match, once normal proceedings had resumed in late September, was Ireland's visit to Murrayfield, a ground they hadn't won on in 16 years, where they lost 10-32 to end their Grand Slam hopes. The Irish then registered their best-ever score against Wales with a 36-6 victory in the Millennium Stadium before welcoming England for the final game of the schedule.

The free-flowing attacking rugby that had been evident in England's first four games was understandably rusty but they still made Ireland work for their victory. There were only two tries in the game – one from Wood, the other by Healey – as it finished 20-14 to the home side. England might have blown the Grand Slam, but they still claimed the Six Nations title.

ENGLAND BEAT AUSTRALIA IN THE WORLD CUP FINAL 2003

Aspirations were high as England started their 2003 World Cup campaign, having won three of the last four Six Nations championships with the most recent seeing them record their 12th Grand Slam title. They went into the tournament as joint favourites with New Zealand, although South Africa and Australia were expected to be strong contenders as usual.

Originally intended to be co-hosted by Australia and New Zealand, the tournament was staged purely in Australia after a dispute over ground signage rights. After a change in qualification for the 1999 World Cup, this time round saw a return to the eight quarter-finalists from the previous tournament gaining automatic entry. The remaining 12 places were fought over by a record 81 nations.

Both Australia and England came through the group stage with a 100% record. The Wallabies cruised to victories over Argentina (24-8), Romania (90-8) and Namibia (142-0) before emerging victorious from a close-fought encounter with Ireland (17-16). England, meanwhile, qualified with wins over Georgia (84-6), South Africa (25-6), Samoa (35-22) and Uruguay (111-13) to set up a quarter-final clash with Wales.

The Welsh put up a good fight and scored three tries – Stephen Jones, Colin Charvis and Martyn Williams – but it was the boot of Jonny Wilkinson that did the damage, scoring six penalties, a drop goal and converting Will Greenwood's try. Australia found themselves paired with Scotland but eased into the semi-finals with tries from Stirling Mortlock, George Gregan and David Lyons giving them a 33-16 triumph.

The semi-finals saw two northern hemisphere teams and two southern hemisphere sides pitched against each other as Australia faced the All Blacks while England took on France. The Wallabies had the boot of Elton Flatley to thank for their 22-10 win while England relied totally on Wilkinson's kicking to secure their 24-7 victory with five penalties and three drop goals. This set up a repeat of the 1991 final, that Australia had won 12-6.

The final itself took place in Sydney's Telstra Stadium on 22 November 2003 and Australia put the first points on the scoreboard when winger Lote Tuqiri outjumped Jason Robinson to catch a Stephen

ENGLAND BEAT AUSTRALIA IN THE WORLD CUP FINAL

Larkham up and under after just six minutes. Fly-half Jonny Wilkinson soon had England in front with two penalties before the Whites were presented with a try-scoring opportunity. Unfortunately, Ben Kay failed to collect the ball from Matt Dawson's pass and knocked on when it seemed easier to score.

Following a third Wilkinson penalty, England moved further in front when Lawrence Dallaglio made ground before passing to Wilkinson who found Robinson steaming up on his left shoulder. The pass was timed to perfection and Robinson registered the second try of the game to send England in with a half-time lead of 14-5.

The second half, however, saw the Australians put nine points on the board with England failing to add to their tally. As can so often be their undoing, England gave away two needless penalties which allowed Elton Flatley to close the gap to three points. Then, with 90 seconds of normal time left on the clock, England were penalised for collapsing a scrum and Flatley levelled the match to send the game into extra-time.

After Wilkinson had again put England in front with another penalty, Australia were awarded a penalty of their own after England held on to the ball on the floor with two minutes to go and Flatley equalised at 17-17. Then came the moment that every England fan will remember for the rest of their lives and that every Australian cannot wait to forget.

With just over one minute remaining on the clock, England won a line-out and drove towards the Australian line. Everybody in the stadium knew that they were waiting to give Wilkinson the opportunity to kick for goal. The fly-half, the youngest member of the squad, had already missed two drop goal attempts but still had enough confidence to try again.

Three times England tried to drive through the Australian defence before Dawson decided to pass back to Wilkinson who was sitting in the pocket. The England number 10 kept a cool head and gave a perfect demonstration of how to kick a drop goal. The ball flew through the posts with just 28 seconds left on the clock and England had won the World Cup before the match went to a sudden-death decision.

Martin Johnson lifted the William Webb Ellis trophy but England suffered a torrid time over the next few years, finishing third and fourth in the following two Six Nations championships and embarking on a seven-match losing streak in 2006. Wilkinson himself suffered a series of injuries and didn't play for his country after the World Cup final until February 2007 when he inspired England to victory in the Calcutta Cup match against Scotland.

WASPS BEAT TOULOUSE IN THE HEINEKEN CUP FINAL 2004

London Wasps completed the Double of Zurich Premiership and Heineken Cup in May 2004, matching the feat of Leicester Tigers in 2000-01 and 2001-02. They became the fourth English side to win the European trophy with their 27-20 victory over Toulouse, following in the footsteps of Leicester, Bath (1997-98) and Northampton (1999-2000). It also meant that England had claimed five titles during the competition's first nine years (France won three and Ireland one).

Toulouse were the defending Heineken Cup champions, having defeated Perpignan by 22-17 at Dublin's Lansdowne Road the previous year. They had also won the trophy in its inaugural year, beating Cardiff Blues by 21-18 at Cardiff Arms Park in 1995-96. While London Wasps did not have the same European pedigree as the French side, they had enjoyed sustained domestic success with three English titles (1989-90, 1996-97 and 2002-03). They had also been runners-up on three occasions in the late 1980s and early 1990s and had claimed the Parker Pen Challenge Cup in 2002-03.

The showpiece final was held at Twickenham for the second time in the competition's history but it was the French side who opened the scoring after seven minutes. Fly-half Yann Delaigue successfully kicked a penalty awarded after Wasps had infringed at a ruck on the 22m line. The same player then added a further three points, taking his team to a 6-0 lead, after the English side had been penalised for pulling down the scrum yet again.

Wasps responded by pushing deep into their opponents' half and were rewarded with a penalty after referee Alain Rolland spotted French hands in the ruck. Full-back Mark Van Gisbergan made no mistake with his kick and halved Toulouse's advantage. Now that Wasps had the taste for scoring, it wasn't long before they registered their first try. Van Gisbergan and Simon Shaw combined on the right-hand side before Howley fed the ball inside to Stuart Abbott who sped over the line for five points. Van Gisbergan succeeded with the conversion to give his side a 10-6 lead.

This only served to spur the French side on and they responded with a failed drop goal attempt from Delaigue before Josh Lewsey beat Emile Ntamack to a bouncing Jauzion kick to touch down

WASPS BEAT TOULOUSE IN THE HEINEKEN CUP FINAL

behind his own line. The referee, meanwhile, pulled play back and awarded Toulouse another penalty which Delaigue failed to convert. Van Gisbergan wasn't in such a charitable mood, however, and slotted a 45-yard penalty through the posts just after the half-hour mark to give his team a seven-point lead. There was still time for Delaigue to touch down a bouncing ball that had been chipped over the Wasps' defending line and – having missed the conversion – send his side into the interval just 11-13 down.

The second half had barely kicked off before Van Gisbergan collected a pass from Alex King on the French 22m line before sprinting through a tackle by Finau Maka. With the full-back also adding the two points from the conversion, Wasps now led 20-11. Delaigue had two further chances to reduce the deficit before he was substituted. In the 47th minute he missed another penalty and three minutes later fluffed another attempted drop goal before being replaced by Jean-Baptiste Elissalde.

Following Lawrence Dallaglio's yellow card, the replacement kicker made no mistake with his first opportunity and scored a penalty that left his team just six points behind their opponents. When King saw his attempted drop goal hit the post and Elissalde successfully converted another penalty after a line-out infringement, it seemed that Wasps might be running out of luck. This seemed to be confirmed when Van Gisbergan missed a long penalty.

Both the crowd and the players were temporarily distracted by a streaker before Elissalde brought his side level with his third penalty just four minutes from time. But there was still time left for one more score and it went to Wasps. Rob Howley received the ball on Toulouse's 22m line and kicked the ball towards the try-line. It bounced along the ground and full-back Clement Poitrenaud was undecided as to whether the ball would bounce into touch or over the try-line so he hesitated. This allowed Howley to complete his sprint and dive onto the ball.

There was an anxious wait while the referee consulted his colleague who viewed replays of the move and eventually confirmed it was a try. Van Gisbergan successfully converted, albeit off the upright, and Wasps had won their first Heineken Cup trophy.

Six days later, they were back at the home of English rugby to complete their Double with a 10-6 victory over Bath with Abbott scoring the only try of the game. While they were unable to successfully defend their Heineken Cup title the following year, they did retain their status as Zurich Premiership champions with a 39-14 win over Leicester Tigers.

LEICESTER TRIUMPH OVER LONDON IRISH 39-22
2004

When Leicester Tigers turned up to play London Irish at the Madejski Stadium in Reading on 19 September 2004, little did they know they were about to rewrite the history books. Martin Corry crossed the home team's goal-line after 26 seconds of the match to record the fastest-ever try in the Zurich Premiership.

Leicester – formed in 1880 – were the most successful English club of the professional era so far and had completed the Double of the Premiership title and Heineken Cup in 2000-01 and 2001-02. London Irish, on the other hand, could only claim the 2002 Powergen Cup to their name. Also known as the Exiles, the club was formed in 1898 for young Irish people of London and the team follows the lines of its older siblings London Welsh and London Scottish.

Leicester's perfect start came when the Exiles' number 8 Kieran Roche mishandled the ball following a high kick-off from Andy Goode. The ball was quickly moved right to Geordan Murphy who aimed for a gap in the defending line before releasing Corry who scored with just 26 seconds on the clock. The conversion was slotted over by Goode for a 7-0 lead. Murphy was the weak link in the Tigers' next scoring opportunity, however, being unable to hold onto a pass from Seru Rabeni when he had plenty of support outside.

London Irish had by now recovered from the shock of conceding so early on in the game and began to fashion their own attacks. This resulted in them being awarded a penalty which Barry Everitt duly dispatched while Tigers captain Martin Johnson was being shown the yellow card and extended an invitation to the sin bin. His punishment would unusually last almost 14 minutes rather than the regulation 10. In a game of ebb and flow, it was the Tigers' turn to advance and they stole the ball from a scrum on their opponents' 22m line. Goode fed the ball to Rabeni who made no mistake and touched down to give his side a 12-3 advantage. But Leicester started giving away needless penalties and before too long the home side had edged into a 15-12 lead.

When Austin Healey charged down an attempted clearance, Murphy quickly collected the ball and headed for the try-line. Facing a mêlée of defenders, he chipped the ball as he entered the Irish

22 but was tackled just short of the line. Support soon arrived in the form of Brett Deacon who dived over the line to restore the Tigers' advantage. Goode slotted home the conversion to send the visitors into the interval with a 19-15 lead.

The home side put in a determined effort after the break, but it was Leicester who scored first. Daryl Gibson's superb run ended in referee Wayne Barnes awarding a penalty which Goode duly converted to extend Leicester's lead to seven points. Although Gibson limped off soon after, Goode scored his side's fourth try to claim the bonus point (the Zurich Premiership scoring system offered four points for a win, plus the added incentive of a bonus point for any team that scores four or more tries). The move had started with the fly-half before the ball had passed through the hands of Neil Back, Martin Corry and Louis Deacon before going to ground. Goode collected the loose ball and touched down before adding the conversion to set the scores at 29-15.

They did not enjoy this advantage for long, as London Irish hit back almost immediately through a well-worked Scott Staniforth try after 63 minutes. With Everitt converting, the deficit was again reduced to seven points. Unfortunately for the home side, they were not able to score any more points.

Leicester, however, were happy to keep racking the score up. Austin Healey was on the end of an intricate three-man move following a line-out to score Leicester's fifth try in the 68th minute and Goode added the conversion and a further penalty five minutes from time to give a final score of 39-22 to the Tigers.

Exiles coach Gary Gold said after the game that "we have lived with Leicester's physicality before but we need to have that physicality for 80 minutes, not 50 minutes, which is not just good enough."

Tigers' coach John Wells was understandably in a much better mood. "I'm delighted with the performance," he said. "To come away from home and get five points – I think the lads are pretty pleased with themselves and so they should be, to come here and win is a great result."

Leicester went on to have a good season, finishing first in the Zurich Premiership league table – though they lost the championship final against London Wasps 14-39 – and reaching the semi-final of the Heineken Cup where they were defeated 19-27 by eventual winners Toulouse.

WALES WIN THE SIX NATIONS 2005

Although Wales had won the Five Nations championship in 1979 (and the Triple Crown), 1988 (again with the Triple Crown but the championship had to be shared with France) and 1994, they had not registered a Grand Slam title since 1978. Their fortunes had waned following the retirement of key players like Gareth Edwards and Phil Bennett at the end of the 1978 campaign.

Indeed, the once-mighty Red Dragons had even ended up with the wooden spoon as recently as 2003 when they failed to win a single game. This season, however, would prove to be a return to the glory days as Wales became the first team to win a Grand Slam by winning more games on their travels rather than at the Millennium Stadium.

The campaign kicked off with a game against the old enemy in Cardiff. With England making uncharacteristic mistakes Wales took advantage, winning a line-out, moving the ball first right and then left before Shane Williams dashed over the line to score the only try of the game. With the try not converted, England's Charlie Hodgson reduced the deficit to two points when they were awarded a penalty.

Stephen Jones restored Wales' five-point advantage before the game turned ugly when Danny Grewcock caught scrum-half Dwayne Peel in the face with his boot and Welsh captain Gareth Thomas retaliated. Both were shown yellow cards.

After the interval, Hodgson scored two penalties (on 48 and 70 minutes) to put England ahead for the first time in the match but the visitors hadn't counted on Gavin Henson, who successfully kicked a long-range penalty in the dying minutes. The 11-9 scoreline gave his side their first home win over England for 12 years. The other results that weekend saw France beat Scotland 16-9 and Ireland triumph over Italy by 28-17.

Wales travelled to Italy and returned with their first away win in almost four years. Tries from Jonathan Thomas, Tom Shanklin, Martyn Williams, Brent Cockbain, Shane Williams and Robert Sidoli together with four conversions from Stephen Jones gave the Welshmen a convincing 38-8 victory in Rome. Luciano Orquera scored the Azzurri's consolation try, with De Marigny

WALES WIN THE SIX NATIONS

adding a second-half penalty. In the weekend's two other games, Scotland fell 13-40 to Ireland at Murrayfield while England narrowly lost 17-18 to France at Twickenham.

The Red Dragons' third match saw them pitted against France – Grand Slam winners themselves in 2002 and 2004 – in Paris and, with France scoring two early tries, it looked as if a drubbing might be on the cards. Dimitri Yachvili scored the first after just four minutes and added the conversion before a mistake by Henson allowed the French to score again through Aurelien Rougerie. Stephen Jones put Wales on the scoresheet with a penalty after 23 minutes before Yachvili restored their 12-point advantage.

Jones added another penalty as Wales went into half-time 6-15 down. Two second-half tries from Martyn Williams turned the match around and Wales recorded an historic 24-18 victory. Elsewhere, Scotland beat Italy 18-10 while Ireland kept their Grand Slam hopes alive by beating England 19-13.

Scotland were the Dragons' next victims as Wales cruised to a record 46-22 victory at Murrayfield. Two tries from Kevin Morgan plus one apiece from Ryan Jones, Rhys Williams and Shane Williams – five of which were converted by Stephen Jones – helped the visitors to a 38-3 half-time lead. Although Scotland came out stronger and more determined after the interval – with Andy Craig, Rory Lamont and Chris Paterson scoring tries – Rhys Williams crossed the line for his second touchdown which, together with another penalty from Jones, secured Wales' victory. In the other results, England beat Italy 39-7 while Ireland lost 19-26 at home to France.

With the final three games all being played on the same day but at differing kick-off times, France needed Wales to lose while they themselves registered a big score to keep their hopes of a Six Nations title alive and they scored seven tries in Rome as they cruised to a 53-16 triumph over Italy (England beat Scotland 43-22).

To the delight of a capacity crowd in Cardiff who had been treated to Max Boyce singing a new verse of "Hymns And Arias" written especially for the day, Wales held their nerve to claim their first Grand Slam in 28 years. Tries in each half from Gethin Jenkins and Kevin Morgan together with five penalties (four from Jones plus a huge 52m kick from Henson) and a Henson drop goal secured a 32-20 victory that sparked massive celebrations around the Principality. Ireland scored two tries through Marcus Horan and Geordan Murphy.

Unfortunately, with expectations riding high, Wales were not able to continue their revival and finished fifth in the following season's Six Nations with just one win (28-18 against Scotland) and a draw (18-18 at home to Italy) to show for their efforts.

MUNSTER BEAT BIARRITZ 23-19 AND WIN THE HEINEKEN CUP 2006

Following their defeats at the hands of Northampton Saints (8-9 in 1999-2000) and Leicester Tigers (9-15 in 2001-02), Munster finally made it third time lucky in the 2005-06 Heineken Cup final. Matched against French opposition in Biarritz Olympique, they finally bagged their first European trophy in Cardiff's Millennium Stadium.

Munster, founded in 1879, can claim to be the only Irish side to have beaten the All Blacks when they emerged victorious from a Halloween meeting in 1978 with a 12-0 scoreline. That was the only match New Zealand lost on their tour of the British Isles, including games against England, Ireland, Scotland and Wales. Not even the national side can boast such an impressive result, with their best showing being a 10-10 draw at Lansdowne Road in 1973. As well as winning the Irish Inter-Pro championship on 22 occasions, Munster have also claimed the Celtic League title (2002-03) and the Celtic Cup (2004-05).

Biarritz, on the other hand, can trace their origins back to 1902 and have had two periods of success in their 100-plus year history. They won the French championship twice in the 1930s (1935 and 1939) but have enjoyed a renaissance period since the start of the 21st century. They have since added three more national titles to their trophy cabinet, in 2002, 2005 and 2006. They list some famous French internationals among the players who have graced their colours including Serge Betsen, Serge Blanco, Dimitri Yachvili and Philippe Bernat-Salles.

The match kicked off and the French side immediately won possession, with Julien Peyrelougne kicking for touch but Munster won the line-out and Ronan O'Gara cleared. This reprieve didn't last long, however, as Biarritz counter attacked in a move that ended with Sereli Bobo scoring the first try of the game. Yachvili converted and Olympique gained a 7-0 lead. Three minutes later, Biarritz were penalised for pulling down a maul and O'Gara scored Munster's first three points from the resulting penalty kick. The Irish side were now finding their feet and mounting sustained attacks on Biarritz and this paid off in the 17th minute when Trevor Halstead succeeded in touching down following a pass from Denis Leamy. O'Gara converted to give Munster a 10-7 advantage.

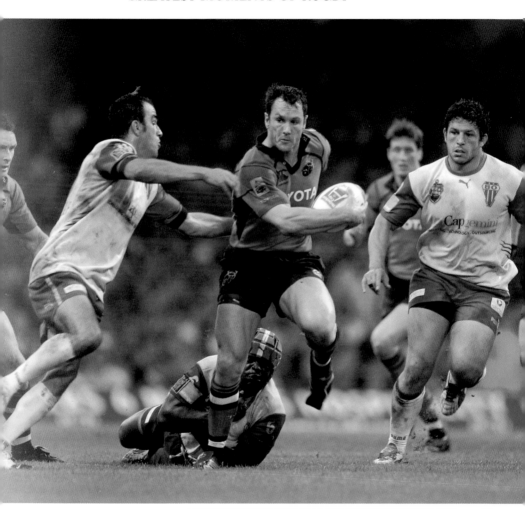

MUNSTER BEAT BIARRITZ 23-19 AND WIN THE HEINEKEN CUP

It was Munster's turn to concede a penalty five minutes later following a ruck and Yashvili levelled the scores with a well-taken kick. The middle period of the first half saw the Irishmen exert their dominance over the game. While Biarritz did have a spell of pressure, it was Munster who scored the next points. A kick by O'Gara intended for the corner only found the French 22m line but from a resulting scrum Peter Stringer fooled the opposition and, instead of feeding the ball left as expected, scored a marvellous individual try after spotting a gap on the blindside. O'Gara successfully kicked the conversion and, after another encampment in the French half, Munster went into half-time with a 17-10 lead.

The second half started where the first had left off, with Munster on the attack. The second period was only two minutes old when O'Gara kicked another three points for the Irishmen after referee Chris White spotted an infringement by the Biarritz players following Stringer's high kick. Six minutes later, Yachvili reduced the deficit to 20-13 after Horgan was adjudged to be offside.

The French scrum-half cut Munster's advantage to just four points minutes later after Imanol Harinordoquy was high-tackled. The game ebbed and flowed after this with both sides trying to gain an advantage but finding that play was breaking down before either could get into a scoring position and it wasn't until the 70th minute that further points were notched up.

Captain Anthony Foley was penalised in a ruck and that handed Yachvili the opportunity to bring Olympique to within one point of their opponents, which he gratefully accepted to set up a nail-biting last 10 minutes. Biarritz gave away a needless penalty when Census Johnson entered a ruck from the side and O'Gara scored his third penalty of the game to ease Munster ahead with a four-point cushion.

The last few minutes proved to be both scrappy and nervous as Biarritz desperately tried to find a way through the Irish defence. In the last minute, they won a scrum deep inside the Munster half but the pressure was relieved when Bobo was hauled up for being accidentally offside. With O'Gara's clearing kick from the scrum, the referee blew for full-time and the 60,000 Irish fans inside the stadium began to celebrate.

The members of the Irish bench ran onto the pitch to join in the celebrations while the giant video screen showed what was happening back in the Limerick streets. Munster, who had progressed to the knockout stages in every tournament since 1998, were finally crowned kings of Europe.

NEW ZEALAND DOMINATE INTERNATIONAL SERIES
2006

With less than 12 months to go before the sixth World Cup, New Zealand showed they were in perfect form with the carefully executed demolition of England, France and Wales in the 2006 autumn internationals.

The All Blacks had won the inaugural tournament in 1987 but had flattered to deceive in each subsequent competition. They lost the 1995 final despite the awesome form of winger Jonah Lomu but had fallen at the semi-final stage in each of the other three tournaments.

Their first match of the tour was against England at Twickenham on Bonfire Night with fly-half Dan Carter opening the scoring with a penalty. England quickly regrouped and mounted an attack on the All Blacks' try-line. With Martin Corry twice making ground, the ball ended up with Jamie Noon who was tackled by Ma'a Nonu and Chris Jack just short of the line. Noon attempted to roll over the line and ground the ball but the two New Zealanders did their utmost to prevent him from achieving this. Referee Joel Jutge had to rely on video replays before giving his decision and it was one that disappointed the majority of the 82,000 crowd as it proved inconclusive as to whether the ball was actually touched down.

After Carter had converted his second penalty, Aaron Mauger crossed the line for the first try of the game, which the All Blacks fly-half duly converted to give his side a 13-0 advantage. Noon did, however, manage a try that was allowed to score five points for his side just before the half-hour mark but the Kiwis effectively sealed the match before half-time. Anthony Allen's pass was intercepted by Joe Rokocoko in his own half and the winger sprinted more than half the length of the pitch to score his side's second try while Carl Hayman added another just before the interval as New Zealand went in with a 28-5 lead.

In the second half, England put up more of a fight and scored tries through Ben Cohen and Shaun Perry but the match belonged to Dan Carter who went on to score a record-breaking 26 points – including a try of his own – as New Zealand totalled the most number of points conceded by England at home to run out 41-20 winners.

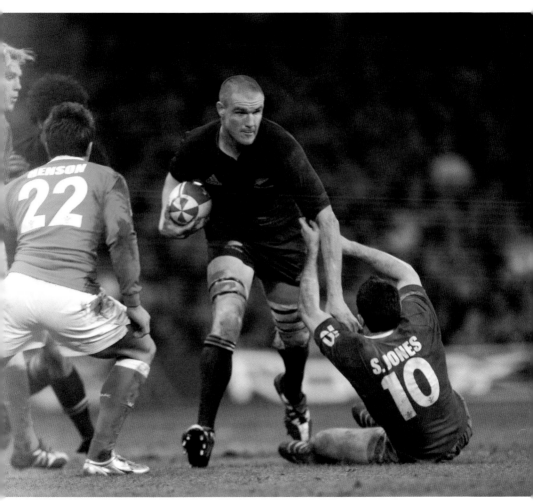

The tourists then played France twice in a week, thrashing the Cockerels 47-3 at Lyon's Stade de Gerland and winning a closer-fought encounter in Paris by 23-11. The first match, played on Armistice Day, could not have been more of a slaughter, with the All Blacks notching up a record victory over the French with tries from Sivivatu (2), Carter, McAlister, McCaw, Rokococo and Smith taking advantage of captain Fabien Pelous being sin binned for 10 minutes.

The French made things more difficult for the visitors in the second Test a week later. Despite the home side scoring the first try of the game through Heymans, the All Blacks retaliated with tries from Nonu and Rokococo. Carter added another 13 points with three penalties and two conversions as the Kiwis established their dominance over the current Six Nations title holders.

In the final match of their tour, New Zealand faced Wales at the Millennium Stadium in a match that proved to be controversial even before a ball was kicked. Confusion had reigned over the order of the pre-match schedule, with Wales wanting to sing "Hen Wlad fy Nhadau" after the All Blacks had performed their ritual prior to kick-off. (New Zealand granted Wales their wish of performing the national anthem immediately before kick-off the previous year as part of the WRU's centenary celebrations). Unfortunately, the Kiwis took affront at the same scheduling so decided to perform the Haka in their dressing room and not, as is traditional, on the pitch.

The match started off with the All Blacks intent on destroying their opponents and Luke McAlister scored the first try after just four minutes following a counter attack after Stephen Jones had failed to find touch. Carter converted and added three penalties to give his side a 16-0 lead with just 20 minutes on the clock. Jones did register three points with a penalty but if the Welsh faithful thought that this was the start of a comeback, they were sadly mistaken. Sitiveni Sivivatu scored the first of his three tries shortly afterwards following a one-on-one with Tom Shanklin with a second following just before the break to send his side in with a 28-3 lead.

The second half saw much of the same and, although Martyn Williams scored a try for the home side, Wales were comprehensively beaten 45-10. While not a record winning margin for the All Blacks in Cardiff, it was a record number of points scored, and it ensured that Wales were still awaiting their first victory over New Zealand since their 13-8 victory in December 1953.

ALL BLACKS WIN WORLD CUP AT LAST

2011

On their home soil the All Blacks at last put their 24-year nightmare behind them as they beat France 8-7 in the lowest scoring Rugby World Cup final ever.

When captain Richie McCaw raised the Webb Ellis Cup, the capacity Eden Park crowd of 61,000 - and a nation of four million supporters - bellowed their adoration and breathed a collective sigh of relief.

The torment which had followed the All Blacks for the past five tournaments had been erased and the team – coached by Graham Henry – proved they were worthy winners and the best team of the tournament.

The game was no push over though. France came to play, and made their intentions clear just before kick off as they challenged the Haka in a unique and somewhat controversial way.

Wearing their white away strip, France linked arms and formed a 'flying V' before marching menacingly towards the All Blacks, making it clear they weren't going to simply make up the numbers in this their third RWC final.

"I wasn't alone, I had my teammates with me. I felt them close to me — too close at one stage, because they wanted to go across the field and hug New Zealand," said captain Thierry Dusautoir.

"It was necessary to calm them down. But it's a great moment that we'll all remember. I felt during the week that the players wanted to do something during the haka, like they did in 2007. "

Prop Fabien Barcella was one of the Frenchman who continued forward, having to be held back at times. "It was a 'V' for victory, quite simply. It was the chance of a lifetime to play a final at Eden Park, we didn't want to miss out on it. It came from the heart, and showed that the 30 of us were together that night."

Francois Trinh-Duc, the fly-half who started off of the bench, said that the players

ALL BLACKS WIN WORLD CUP AT LAST

needed to make an impression on their opponents: "We had to throw down the challenge to them. It was a way of defying them, letting them know we were there. I think they were surprised, they weren't expecting it. "

Indeed, France gave them a greater scare than anyone imagined. Similar to the sides' pool match, the French held possession for large chunks of the opening period until Piri Weepu made a significant impact.

He won a turnover penalty and then kicked 50 metres downfield to a lineout where the All Blacks pulled out a piece of practice-ground magic. Keven Mealamu lobbed the delivery to the back where Jerome Kaino passed it down to Tony Woodcock who charged over the try-line.

Weepu missed the conversion and all three of his attempts in the opening half which left the All Blacks without much of a buffer at the break.

The French had their troubles too: Morgan Parra was battered by a Ma'a Nonu charge which signalled his exit from the test after 22 minutes.

Kieran Read was piling on the pressure for the French with his charging runs in midfield, breaking the advantage line with every foray and giving Weepu options either side of the rucks.

The French clung on resolutely, trusting their defence would hold and they could ride out the assaults. After half an hour they hadn't conceded any more points and began to string several phases together.

They also watched the All Blacks lose Aaron Cruden to injury when he was sandwiched in a double tackle and hyper-extended his right knee.

His misfortune brought Stephen Donald on to the park, a squad replacement and the fourth-choice pivot making his first tournament appearance in the World Cup final.

GREATEST MOMENTS OF RUGBY

The tension was palpable in the stadium and it was spreading to the players at the break. There was some respite when Donald took over the kicking duties and landed a 36 metre penalty but the French were not done.

Weepu made a careless hack at a loose ball from the base of a ruck and only succeeded in chipping it into the hands of replacement five-eighths Francois Trinh-Duc.

He weaved downfield and with Aurelien Rougerie in support, France worked their way towards the line and, the defence outflanked, captain Thierry Dusautoir strolled across.

Trinh-Duc kicked the conversion and the All Black selectors sent Weepu and Sam Whitelock to the cooler.

Thirty minutes were left, France had the momentum and somehow the All Blacks had to find an antidote. They struggled.

Trinh-Duc missed a 48 metre penalty but France pushed on. Israel Dagg lost the ball in a mid-air leap near his 22 and Andy Ellis's kick was charged down.

The All Blacks needed to play territory. Dagg found some with a deep kick then Donald squeezed a smart kick downfield. But France countered with their lineout where they had at least five jumpers and dominated the air.

Ten minutes left and France still came forward. The All Blacks used all their defensive clout to repel them. Who would crack in the brutality? Not the All Blacks; not this time.

Eventually referee Craig Joubert stilled their nerves and those of the whole country when he signalled the end of a chilling contest.

The 2011 All Blacks were the World Cup winners, champions of the world, the elite class to stand alongside their 1987 predecessors.

WALES BEAT FRANCE TO WIN GRAND SLAM
2012

Wales's victory over France on the final day of the 2012 RBS Six Nations delivered an 11th Grand Slam on the back of a 20th Triple Crown three weeks earlier.

The campaign began with a stunning 21-23 victory over Ireland at the Aviva Stadium when Leigh Halfpenny converted a late penalty to use Wales's get out of jail card for the tournament.

Ireland appeared to have grabbed the game by the scruff of the neck when Bradley Davies was yellow carded for a tip tackle. Tommy Bowe scored a try to put Ireland in control while Davies was off the park.

But George North scored in the corner to bring Wales to within a point. With the seconds ticking away, Stephen Ferris was sin binned for a debatable tip tackle on Ian Evans. Halfpenny showed nerves of steel to bang over the winning penalty.

The second round of the championship was more routine with Wales romping to a 27-13 win over Scotland at the Millennium Stadium. All Wales's points were scored by Cardiff Blues players with Alex Cuthbert slicing over while Leigh Halfpenny added a brace along with three conversions and two penalties for a personal haul of 22 points.

Fortress Twickenham was stormed 12-19 with Scott Williams turning the game in the visitor's favour with a brilliant piece of individualism. Leigh Halfpenny and Owen Farrell had levelled the scores 12-12 with their boots when Williams robbed rampaging England lock Courtney Lawes of the ball before kicking ahead and winning the race to the ball to score close to the posts to leave the Twickenham crowd stunned as Wales picked up the Triple Crown.

Phase four was completed with a routine 24-3 triumph over Italy before Wales met France at Cardiff in a winner takes all battle for the Six Nations' championship.

A minute's silence was held before kick-off to pay tribute to former Wales and Lions number eight Mervyn Davies who had died a few days before the match.

The team felt a special desire to win for 'Merv the Swerve' who had captained Wales for their 1976 Grand Slam but it was France who went ahead first through a Dimitri Yachvili penalty.

Fly-half Rhys Priestland's first penalty attempt also rebounded off an upright while Halfpenny received treatment for a knock. But Wales lock Alun Wyn Jones executed a superb steal on the floor from Dusautoir and when the ball went right, Cuthbert cut past Bonnaire some 30 metres out before bursting clear for the opening try after 22 minutes.

Halfpenny added the conversion and after centre Davies's ball-freeing tackle on Florian Fritz, the full-back landed the penalty that resulted from the panic in the visiting defence.

The up-and-unders were coming thick and fast from both teams amid the test of nerves. Overall, however, Wales won the tactical battle in the opening period with greater possession and greater territorial gains.

A Jamie Roberts chip and chase created another Welsh chance as Dan Lydiate and lock Jones followed up to force another penalty, but Halfpenny saw it rebound off an upright to leave them 10-3 ahead at the break.

Wales suffered a blow at that point with skipper Sam Warburton continuing his record of not having finished a game against France, this time because of a shoulder injury.

Ryan Jones, sporting a Mervyn Davies-style headband, came into a reshuffled back-row and Gethin Jenkins took over as captain.

Cuthbert broke through on the counter-attack as Wales began the second period with familiar intent, but just as Beauxis had failed with a long-range drop-goal, Priestland's effort also failed to get off the ground.

Gethin Jenkins illegally halted the threat after Palisson's dangerous chip-and-chase caught Wales out and Beauxis kicked the penalty.

A frenetic period of end-to-end counter-attacking offered Halfpenny the moment he had been craving since a late, long-range penalty attempt fell short in Wales' failed 2011 World Cup quarter-final against France.

This time the full-back's thumping kick crossed the bar with metres to spare to put Wales a converted try ahead with 27 minutes remaining, only for the French defence to come out on top in five-minute arm-wrestle on the visitors' 22 that followed.

Having won that psychological battle, France failed to take advantage when their scrum was caught engaging early in Wales' 22.

Wales also had a let-off when Imanol Harinordoquy failed to spot Louis Picamoles on his right after Halfpenny had lost control near his own line.

Yachvili kicked the penalty that followed, but Halfpenny responded with a brilliant counter-attack that allowed him the chance to kick another penalty.

Priestland saw a late drop-goal attempt skew wide but the home side were in control for the final play to bring down the curtain on their success and secure Wales their third grand slam since 2005.

LIONS WIN THIRD TEST TO BEAT AUSTRALIA
2013

While the Lions convincing 41-16 victory over Australia to win the series in the Sydney summer of 2013 can rightly be considered as one of British rugby's 'greatest moments' – it was also one of the worst moments for Irish legend Brian O'Driscoll.

The experienced centre was sensationally dropped by coach Warren Gatland despite having played in the two previous Tests. Gatland could argue that his decision was proved correct as the Lions sealed their first series victory since 1997.

Gatland had summoned some heavy artillery in making six changes to the side that narrowly failed to clinch the three-Test series in Melbourne when Australia edged a 16-15 win, and the changes yielded an immediate reward when one of them, Corbisiero, burrowed over with just one minute and 17 seconds on the clock.

Will Genia knocked on Sexton's kick-off to give the tourists a scrum platform that produced the first in a series of free-kicks and penalties.

Mike Phillips took a quick tap, Alun Wyn Jones was held up short, but the England prop - who missed the second Test through injury - forced his way over at the posts, Halfpenny adding the conversion.

The Lions promised an overtly physical approach, and hooker Richard Hibbard was at the heart of it.

Veteran Australia flanker George Smith, recalled for his first Test in four years, was led off gingerly after a sickening clash of heads with the Welshman in the fifth minute.

Remarkably Smith reappeared five minutes later, by which stage a thumping hit from Dan Lydiate on Joe Tomane, with help from Sean

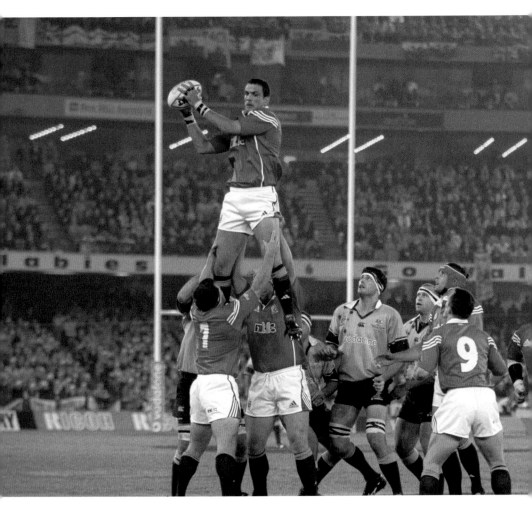

O'Brien, had produced a penalty from which Halfpenny made it 10-0.

Leali'ifano got the hosts on the board from the restart after some deliberate obstruction, but when they were penalised for deliberately wheeling the next scrum, Halfpenny restored the Lions' 10-point lead.

The Wallabies were then driven back on their own ball at the next engagement, with the same result: penalty to the Lions; Halfpenny through the sticks.

Ben Alexander was deemed the culprit, and when referee Romain Poite dispatched the Australia prop to the sin-bin for collapsing another scrum, Halfpenny's fourth successful penalty took him past Jenkins's record from 1997 - the last time the Lions won a series.

Australia belatedly built some momentum as half-time approached, Geoff Parling's superb ankle tap on Jesse Mogg, on as a replacement for the stricken Israel Folau, halting a dangerous attack.

Three times in quick succession Australia opted to kick penalties to touch rather than at goal, each time with no reward. But the third brought a scrum five metres out, and O'Connor stepped past Sexton and O'Brien to squeeze over, Leali'ifano's conversion cutting the deficit to nine points.

That was reduced to three within six minutes of the resumption as Leali'ifano landed two penalties. But after Halfpenny made it 22-16 on 51 minutes, the Lions turned on the style to leave Australia in tatters.

Sexton and Tommy Bowe combined to send Jonathan Davies through a tackle and Halfpenny was on his shoulder, getting his pass away for Sexton to sprint over.

Halfpenny's conversion suddenly gave the scoreline a far more reassuring look from a Lions perspective at 29-16. But it just got better and better.

Halfpenny, one of a record-equalling 10 Welshmen in the starting XV, stepped inside Genia and away from Tomane to send North surging to the left corner for a third try.

And the strains of "Bread of Heaven" were still ringing around the ANZ Stadium when Conor Murray's sweet pass put Roberts over for the fourth.

The Lions emptied their bench, including Richie Gray - the only Scot to feature in the series - as their army of travelling support were able to luxuriate in a thumping victory long before the end.

Hero Halfpenny landed eight from nine kicks to finish with 21 points. That was a new individual record for a Lion in a Test, overtaking the previous mark of 20 points shared by Jonny Wilkinson (in 2005 against Argentina) and Stephen Jones (in 2009 against South Africa). It also took Halfpenny past Neil Jenkins's previous series record of 41 points for the Lions, the Welsh full-back finishing with 49.

While all the pre-match talk had been about midfield selections, it was up front where the game was won, as the Lions dominated and gained valuable momentum through powerful performances from Adam Jones, Richard Hibbard and Alex Corbisiero.

"I thought Alex Corbisiero was Man of the Match. We said all along he was unlucky with selection," said the beleaguered Gatland.

"We spoke about being prepared to go to a place where most players don't put their bodies, to the limit. I think we've played some great rugby on this tour. We were able to put it together tonight in that second half. These guys have done themselves proud, they've done the jersey proud."

JONNY & BRIAN BOW OUT AS WINNERS
2014

We end this selection of 'greatest moments' with not a single match but one week in May 2014.

Although it was a nightmare seven days for Saracens, it was a week which saw one of the most exciting Aviva Premiership Finals that was clinched with a last-minute try, and retirement on a winning note for two of the legends of the modern game in Jonny Wilkinson and Brian O'Driscoll.

The week started well for Jonny when his Toulon side joined an elite group of teams to have successfully defended their Heineken Cup title after they beat Saracens 23-6 at the Millennium Stadium on May 24.

It was also the last game on British soil for Jonny who, typically, contributed 13 points to help the French side seal an emphatic victory.

Both sides started slowly in what was anything but a free-flowing game, but Toulon broke loose to score two fantastic tries, with former Test stars Matt Giteau and Juan Smith both going over.

Wilkinson, best remembered for his last-minute match winning drop goal to win the World Cup for England in 2003, rolled back the years, playing a hand in both tries as well as converting them.

A day short of his 35th birthday, he was faultless from the tee in what was the penultimate game of his career, and managed to slot a trademark drop goal too, with his right (wrong) foot.

"It's a hell of a feeling. I can't say enough how proud I am to be a part of that and a part of this team," he said post match. "We've had a hell of a time and our season's got one more game but this is something I'll take with me for ever. There is a lot of relief, a lot of excitement."

Saracens had another shot at glory the following weekend in the Aviva Premiership Final against Northampton Saints, but their heartbreak continued when they lost with the last play, in the last minute of extra time.

Saracens had led 20-17 in the extra time after Charlie Hodgson had kicked a penalty for a deliberate knock-on. The scoreline had been level at 14-14 at the end of normal time after Saracens had had a second half try from Owen Farrell disallowed for a forward pass.

Saints were in heaven when Alex Waller drove over through a morass of arms and legs while

Saracens hellish week ended in another defeat, with their captain Steve Borthwick calling time on a remarkable career which saw him win 57 caps for England (21 as captain) and play a record 264 Premiership matches.

Meanwhile, on the same day May 31, Brian O'Driscoll also played his last game for his beloved Leinster when they defeated Glasgow Warriors 34-12 in the RaboDirect Pro12 Final at Dublin RDS and became the first team to win back-to-back titles – a seventh trophy in seven seasons.

They did it in style too, scoring four tries, with a brace from Zane Kirchner, a performance that softened the blow of losing O'Driscoll after only 10 minutes with a recurrence of an old calf injury.

For the record, O'Driscoll was the most capped player in rugby union history having played 141 test matches – 133 for Ireland (83 as captain), and eight for the British and Irish Lions.

He scored 46 tries for Ireland and one try for the Lions in 2001, making him the highest try scorer of all time in Irish Rugby. He is the highest scoring centre of all time and holds the Six Nations' record for most tries scored with 26.

If it was bad enough that one of the games' greatest players finished his playing career on this day, Jonny Wilkinson also signed off his remarkable playing career by adding a coveted French Top 14 title to his long list of rugby achievements.

Leading Toulon to an emotional 18-10 victory over Castres in Paris was the perfect send-off for the perfectionist No 10, who last won a domestic championship with Newcastle back in 1998.

Playing in shirts with "Merci Jonny" embroidered on their collars, Toulon relied on their captain's fantastic kicking to secure a first league title since 1992, completing a historic double after their victory over Saracens in the Heineken Cup Final the previous weekend.

Wilkinson – unlike O'Driscoll – played a major part in his team's victory landing four penalties with his favoured left boot and a drop goal from his right; yes, the same one that settled the 2003 World Cup Final in England's favour.

Arguably English rugby best-known superstar, his points records were just phenomenal: 1938 points for Newcastle Falcons in 158 games between 1997 and 2009; 1,243 for Toulon in 88 games between 2009 and 2014; 1,179 for England in 91 international matches and 67 for Lions in six tests.

So by glorious coincidence, the end of the month in May 2014, became one of rugby's 'greatest' and saddest moments when British rugby bid farewell to two giants of the modern game.

**The pictures in this book were provided
courtesy of the following:**

GETTY IMAGES
101 Bayham Street, London NW1 0AG

PA PHOTOS
www.paphotos.com

COLORSPORT
www.colorsport.co.uk

FLICKR
www.flickr.com

WIKICOMMONS
commons.wikimedia.org

Design & Artwork by Scott Giarnese

Published by G2 Entertainment Limited

Publishers: Jules Gammond & Edward Adams

Written by Ian Welch & Jules Gammond